DESIGNED
Illusions
Via Divine Power

Autobiographical Memoirs

34 CHAPTERS
17 POST CHAPTERS

PJ Ricchiuti

Copyright © 2023 **Patrick Ricchiuti Publishing**

All rights reserved. No part of this publication may be reproduced, distributed, or transmitted in any form or by any means, including photocopying, recording, or other electronic or mechanical methods, without the prior written permission of the publisher, except in the case of brief quotations embodied in critical reviews and certain other noncommercial uses permitted by copyright law. For permission requests, write to the publisher, addressed "Attention: Book Rights and Permission," at the address below.

Published in the United States of America

ISBN 978-1-962110-29-7 (SC)
ISBN 978-1-962110-27-3 (HC)
ISBN 978-1-962110-28-0 (Ebook)

Patrick Ricchiuti Publishing
222 West 6th Street
Suite 400, San Pedro, CA, 90731
www.stellarliterary.com

Order Information and Rights Permission:

Quantity sales. Special discounts might be available on quantity purchases by corporations, associations, and others. For details, contact the publisher at the address above.

For Book Rights Adaptation and other Rights Permission. Call us at toll-free 1-888-945-8513 or send us an email at admin@stellarliterary.com.

Patrick Ricchiuti

Autobiographical.

My name is Patrick Ricchiuti, born "Pasquale". It's in the book. I was born in 1938 in a small fishing village of Vasto, Italy, on the edge of the Adriatic Sea.

My time there was always about me and an unknown Power. Yes, an unknown Power and me. In 1945 seven years after being born I opened my eyes being without any knowledge of my past seven years. included close-by were two women. The older woman, dressed in black continued with a nasty look at me. My thought was that I had done something and deserved it. The two women would turned out to be my Mom and Grandma.

My only desire was to leave the confines of my room for the outdoor. Unknown to me World War 2 still raged, but not for me. I experiences only illusions of the war per the DIVINE. The war meant nothing to me, as I never actually experienced its noise, smell or sight. It was never explained to me the goings on of the War. No doubt the war included my town of Vasto and in the Adriatic Sea. I had mental adult knowledge, more than my seven years. One day, I was awakened by intense glitter upon my eyes that seemingly came from a crack in a nearby old door. Awakened, before leaving my room for outside I looked for shoes but there were none. Walking barefoot would not be a problem for me. It would just be part of being without normal senses or needs. I would never try and explain to anyone any of my many "Illusions". My association with The DIVINE Power was always within me as I wrote "Designed Illusions" which came easily for an old man. Not the wordings.

Mom and I came by ship to America in 1946. It was at end of World War 2. I was then about eight years old. The "Ship" was also a trip of Designed Illusions and me, as mom slept on. Did I mention that I spoke, understood and heard only one language- English, It all came about without any training or schooling. Of course, only per DIVINE. It was a help for me once in America, Then, reunited with my father, whom I didn't remember.

My father being born an American citizen but went to Italy with his parents who had chosen to return there from America. My father left Italy for America about five years earlier in my life, to answer America's call to arms (drafted). It would be less than a joyful reunion for me, and me for he. negative son and father relations didn't matter much to me. Many episodes of me alone per the DIVINE Power would forever haunt me. "Designed Illusions Via Divine Power" would be continuous

Contents

CHAPTER 1 First remembrance: Sometime 1945 6
CHAPTER 2 Awakened: Sometime 1945 8
CHAPTER 3 The Scooter Boy: Sometime 1945 10
CHAPTER 4 Vendor Girls: Sometime 1945 12
CHAPTER 5 Birdmen: Sometime 1945 15
CHAPTER 6 The Puddle: Sometime 1945 17
CHAPTER 7 Escape to the Farm: Sometime 1945 19
CHAPTER 8 Aerial "Dogfight": Sometime 1945 22
CHAPTER 9 Return to "Dodge": Sometime 1945 25
CHAPTER 10 Publishing the Envelope: Sometime 1945 27
CHAPTER 11 Last straw: Sometime 1945 29
CHAPTER 12 Enemy within: Sometime 1945 32
CHAPTER 13 My Paper Plane Maker: Sometime 1945 34
CHAPTER 14 The Fireplace: Sometime 1945 38
CHAPTER 15 Announcement: Sometime 1945-46 41
CHAPTER 16 Leaving for America: Sometime 1946 43
CHAPTER 17 Ship of Foolery-Food: Sometime 1946 46
CHAPTER 18 Ship of Foolery-Liberty: Sometime 1946 50
CHAPTER 19 Ship of Foolery-shots: Sometime 1946 54
CHAPTER 20 Port of New York: Sometime 1946 57
CHAPTER 21 Final Leg: Sometime 1946 59
CHAPTER 22 From the frying pan: Sometime 1946 61
CHAPTER 23 Diet By Design: Sometime 1946 65
CHAPTER 24 Personals: Sometime 1947 67
CHAPTER 25 The Foster Boy: Sometime 1947 68

CHAPTER 26	Between rock & hard place: Sometime 1947	69
CHAPTER 27	Blast from the Past: Sometime 1947	72
CHAPTER 28	And Baby Makes Four: Sometime 1947	74
CHAPTER 29	More from the P-Nut: Sometime 1947	76
CHAPTER 30	Chesapeake Bay Trip: Sometime 1948	77
CHAPTER 31	Strangers in the Mix: Sometime 1948	78
CHAPTER 32	Miscellaneous: Sometime 1948	80
CHAPTER 33	Leaving Evil: Sometime 1948	82
CHAPTER 34	Stranger than fiction:	85

CHAPTER 1
First remembrance: Sometime 1945

Upon opening my eyes for the very first time, on my own, not forced upon me, I saw a woman wearing a dress lying on the other side of my bed. Later, opening my eyes again, the first woman was gone replaced by an older woman dressed in black, maybe in mourning. She stood at the end of my bed, wearing a frown directed at me. I can only surmise that the first woman got an inkling that I had awakened. She then fetched another woman to witness the event. The household should have called for some sort of celebration, but it didn't happen.

At the time I hadn't known either woman. Now, I surmise that I had been in a "coma" since birth, since early1938. Then finally, but very briefly, I awoke by my own power for the first time. I don't know my exact age then, but I was old enough to be able to gather and retain information. My guess is that I was nearly seven years old.

Unknown to me then, the two women were my mother and grandmother. I had often wondered if grandmother had given me a smile instead of a frown, would I have then remained awake or, was it all of a much greater plan that no one had control over? I now believe that no earthly person could have made a difference.

The entire time of remembrance as I occupied my room was always bright enough for me to see clearly, although no light source of any kind was visible to me. I never experienced darkness. In the same setting, if all were normal, I probably would have stumbled around in the dark, hunting for a light source. Then, I never gave it a thought. To me my situation was all normal. Until I would be known that nothing was normal for me, but I had to continue on. I went back to my bed, and another sleep cycle, to await another episode. I didn't know then, as I believe now, that it was all "procedure" via a Power not of earth.

What I now know is that I didn't have any normal senses. I know this because I never felt anything that was of my physical being, not even the slightest physical aggravation, even being barefoot. I kept it to myself of the constant abnormalities that I had to witness and never confided anything to the physical people that were the only three family members that I would come to know in Italy.

Moving on with my newly found life. Any adult caring or supervision of me was almost non-existed. I wouldn't learn anything from them. I would learn later that I was persona-non-grata to family members. Now, I can't blame anyone for being non-caring of me as a young boy. I now believe that it was all part of the *"Script"* via DIVINE POWER.

At that time World War2 raged-on in 1945, or about to end. I never gave thought of the war. I didn't suffer what others had suffered be it, hunger, injuries, violence, uncertainties, only, a few instances of "illusions of war". I did have some feelings of loneliness.

CHAPTER 2
Awakened:
Sometime 1945

I was on my bed asleep facing a door. Bright glitter came through the cracks of the weather-beaten wooden door which forced my eyes to open. After I gave some thought, I left the old wooden bed and attempted to open the old door. I wanted to go out, though I didn't know where it would lead and didn't care. I awoke a healthy and vibrant at about 7 years old.

Try as I might, the door wouldn't open. Disappointed, I went back on my bed. I started to lie down again but realized that I didn't know anything of my surroundings. I would take that opportunity to take stock of my room.

The walls were concrete and totally bare. There were no windows and no furniture except a small wooden table and a stool. There was no running water or toilet facility. If I needed to go, it would have to be somewhere else in the house. I had no need of a toilet, even for the year to come. The partition was made up of two parallel walls that created an opening instead of a door to enter and exit the rest of the house. I would never use it, even to sneak a peek at the other part of the house, as I had no interest in venturing there. I may have, or not given thought of the two women that I had once seen and that they were probably there somewhere in the house. They were of no importance to me.

My place had a fireplace that was cold and clean, Bed was totally bare. Any additional clothing for me would probably be somewhere on the other side of the partition.

I wore only what I remember as walking shorts and short sleeve shirt. I didn't see shoes nor put on shoes. It is safe to say that I would stay barefoot. I might have given a fleeting glance down at my bare feet. In any case, I was never bothered being barefoot.

I never gave a thought of anything personal of myself. I wouldn't be able to see my own image until we arrived in America, about a year to come. In Vasto, I never saw a mirror, calendar or clock. If not for all the ventures that I now attribute to the DIVINE POWER, Then, I would probably have died of boredom. I was perplexed at my situation and being alone.

I would never be invited to the other parts of the house by anyone. There was a family member in the house that would see to it…Uncle. No problem for me, I had no desire or need to venture in the rest of the house.

Back to the old stubborn door that led to outside. I then heard scrapping coming from outside as if someone was shoveling snow near the door, but it quickly had ended.. Then, the door opened, but just barely. I continued to watch for more opening of the old door. All progress for the door to open further had ceased. I was perturbed that I had to try and squeeze through such a narrow opening. I was soon outside. I put my face at the opening to look outside. It was a beautiful sunny day, but empty of anything. I desperately wanted to be out. Not enough door opening for me to get through. Then, my first inkling of abnormality. I was sent instantly outside. Stunned, I had to look behind me at the still closed door.

To my knowledge I was outside for the first time. The area I was in, as far as I could see, was totally a sunny day. Nothing was distinguishable except for some concrete at the top of a few close-in buildings Now; I have my doubts. I quickly looked for the person who did the shoveled noise without the snow that helped me out. There was no one to be seen.

I fully expected seeing and hearing shoveling activities everywhere, but no one to be seen anywhere. Everything also was cemetery quiet. No odors of the town, An Italian town without odors??

I felt perfectly comfortable the way I was dressed, with walking shorts and a short sleeve shirt and barefoot. I did give fleeting thought that normally I would require more clothing. I decided not to venture any further. Reluctantly, I went back to my room and my bed. Unknown to me, another "deep sleep" cycle was in store, probably until another episode "presented itself."

CHAPTER 3
The Scooter Boy: Sometime 1945

As I slept, again facing the old door to the outside. Then, bright sunlight came through the cracks, which forced my eyes to open. I've often wondered what if had faced the other way, probably not part of the *plan*. I wasn't eager to try the old door, just to be disappointed, but I had no choice, there was nothing in the room for me. There was no sign of the two women, either.

Up and at the door, I was very surprised and delighted that the door easily open and I was quickly outside and another sunny day. There were structures that I then was able to see. I would say it was a warm day, but I can't. Weather would never be a factor for me. About a block away, I entered a foot carved entrance in the shrubbery leading to some place. It quickly revealed the sight of the Adriatic Sea. I knew nothing of World War2, still active. The Sea was totally calm, no sign of war. Not a single vessel, boat of any kind, No activity and no one to be seen. Everything silent. Disappointed, but undaunted, I began my walk toward anything of interest to me. I thought that at any time I would see people. I gave no thought to anything but seeing some activity. The town appeared to be totally empty. Unknown only to me.

I was soon at another part of the town. I ran out of places to see and was perplexed at the continuing emptiness and silence everywhere. I went back to stare back out at the sea. I couldn't smell the pungent sea air, nor hear the waves crashing on the beach. As I was about to turn around and go elsewhere, I heard the unmistakable sound of metal wheels on a hard surface. A boy about my age was quickly and smoothly approaching me. The boy stopped near me on his sturdy homemade wooden scooter. It made me want one for myself. I asked him that I would like to have one like his, and do you know anyone that would make it for me?" The boy picked up the scooter, turned it over to reveal the ball bearings for its wheels. He pointed to the nearby forest as he told me:

"First, you will need the wheels you can get them out there, out of a crashed airplane"" My jaw must have dropped. The boy got back on his scooter. then quickly and effortlessly pushed himself out of sight. Again, disappointed, I would forget of a scooter for myself and maybe just return to my room. Now, of course, I believe the boy to be an illusion.

Retrospect: Apparently, I had the ability to understand things that a long pent-up kid couldn't possibly know. With what the scooter boy said and crashed airplane that I could easily visualize a crumbled heap of metal that may have been thoroughly scavenged and only sharp pieces awaited anyone foolish to enter the crashed airplane. Scooter Boy had pushed himself effortlessly on the town's decrepit street. The Sooter Boy" and I conversed. I shouldn't have been able to converse at all. I had no training of any kind. I could have been a total idiot. However, two Italian kids "spoke" to each other not in Italian, but in fluid English. I would never speak or understand any other language, including Italian. I would never question it to anyone or myself. More Designed Illusions.

CHAPTER 4
Vendor Girls: Sometime 1945

Walking only to continue checking out my town of Vasto. I then saw two early teenage girls each with trays slung from their shoulders. To me, they were "Vendor Girls" I thought they were selling things, but to whom? There was no one else to be seen.

I went over to the girl nearest to me and asked her: What are you doing? "She replied: "Selling things to the American soldiers". I then had to ask her: Can I do what you're doing?" She told me, "First you will need things to sell, then you will need a tray; you can use my extra tray!" She pointed to a tray on the ground, I was then able to sneak a peek at her tray and saw what appeared to be two plump pastries. It gave me some idea of what I would need to sell.

Why would she have an extra tray? Maybe, someone else was using it then gave it up. I could see why, there were no others anywhere. On the other hand, maybe the tray is in keeping with the story.

I picked up the tray and placed the strap firmly on my shoulders. I felt no discomfort from it at all. I still walked barefoot feeling no discomfort. Then, I just happened to see a lone, short and skinny American soldier in his dress uniform, but without a weapon. He was sitting on some steps. How did I know that he was American? Again, I knew more than I should have, considering my situation, or I found it out years later in America. The soldier seemingly had no interest in us. The other Vendor Girl" then left us.

Walking back to my room with the tray firmly around my shoulders, I gave some thought of the two women that I had once seen at some time in the past. Otherwise, I knew of no one that would make the pastries or anything for me. I thought that at least I had the tray just in case, then thought that I was overstepping my bounds. I was starting to regret getting involved.

I was about to reach my bedroom's side door when a woman came rushing out, seemingly eager to confront me. She clearly showed that she was angry. "Where have you been?" she demanded. I didn't know who she was, but I did recognize her dress. I recognized the same dress on my bed when I opened my eyes for the first time, on my own. Meaning, that I don't know in my nearly past seven years that I was in a "coma," like state how often someone had tried to awaken me for whatever purpose. I don't remember it. I surmised that it would be someone who also lived in the house.

I didn't know how to answer her. I went right to the problem at hand and quickly asked of her, "Can you make things to sell to the American soldiers?" She gave me a suspicious cold stare. "I'll try!" she snapped and immediately returned inside. I stood there dumfound that she didn't tell me how long I was expected to wait. Why didn't she take me inside with her? I expected a long wait. The good thing, I still didn't feel the tray on me at all. I could have stood there as long as it took to receive her pastries.

In short order, she returned. I couldn't believe that she made things to sell in such little time. She snapped, "Here!" then, put her offerings on the tray and quickly returned inside the house. Her offering was four small things, no bigger than Hershey Kisses. Immediately, I thought that I couldn't sell them, especially to the American soldiers, should I see another. I was greatly disappointed with the woman, and I thought that it would have been best for her to deny my help request.

The lone American soldier was still sitting at the same spot. He still didn't want to look at me. I ate one of the puny things. Very sweet, I thought, and then I ate two more, they were no more than sugar balls. I looked toward the soldier maybe try and sell one to him. I pressed him for eye contact, and then he did look at me, but with a frown. I got it he didn't want to be bothered.

I walked back toward my room. I didn't expect the woman to come out again. She did and with the same anger. "Where's the money!" she demanded. I couldn't believe that she expected me to sell them. My reply was to eat the remaining two sugar balls in front of her. Upon seeing it, and without another word, she rushed back inside. My room was a short cut to the main part of the house.

Walking back to the square to return the tray, the lone soldier was no longer there either. Both vendor girls were gone. I took off the tray and just wanted to hurl it. I showed impatience early on. Instead, I put it down exactly where I got it. Again, no other "bothersome person" was to be seen, anywhere.

I walked back to my room and probably back to my bed. I would never remember opening that door to my room, walking inside and lying on the bed. Unknown to me still. Per *Designed Illusions*.

CHAPTER 5
Birdmen:
Sometime 1945

I have absolutely no remembrance of anything since the "vendor girls" episode. Next recall, I stopped abruptly as my face was inches from smashing into a brick wall. Confused and scared for the first time. I knew nothing of where I was, where I was going, or where I had come from, but probably from my room, I thought. As I was just about to turn around, shadows at the very top of a building surrendered images of people there moving about. I was overjoyed that it gave me some purpose being there. I wanted to check-out the moving about in that building. My search for the buildings opening was quickly realized. The high concrete spiraling steps were challenging for my short legs. I was beginning to feel claustrophobic and a little panicky going up the many steps and the spiraling narrow wall. The thought of going back down entered my mind but continued. My interest was more important than my temporary fear. Any discomfort was only in my mind I thought. I was still barefoot. As I continued to the top severe knee pain came about. My thought of ending the climb to unknown entered my thoughts.

Continuing seemed all worthwhile. I finally stood at the opening not wanting to be a problem to the two men who were engaged in another activity new to me. Neither one gave me a glance. I wouldn't ask either one to get involved with me I had learned my lesson. From then on, I just wanted to enjoy doing kid stuff, but little chance of that. I wouldn't get the slightest acknowledgement from either man. Was I invisible to them?

The activity: Each man had a long pole. Attached to the tip of their poles was about fifteen feet of string. At the other end of the string was fashioned a noose. The noose was camouflaged with feathers. The constant breeze from the nearby Adriatic Sea sent the feathered noose high in the air. The fluttering feathers in the noose attracted the birds of certain species. One flew in the noose. The "birdman" upon seeing it, pulled on the pole. The noose tightened around the bird, and it was hopelessly caught. It struggled to free itself, but to no avail. The "birdman" with perfected technique, quickly brought the bird down to him. He quickly dispatched it by twisting its neck. The birdman put the dead bird in a pouch attached to his belt. Much like fishing, it was for food and sport, but was it mostly illusions for my eyes only?

The birds were only about twice the size of a sparrow. I continued to watch for another catch. The few other birds might have been scared off upon seeing one of their own caught. The sky was then empty of birds. It might have been then, as now, the problem of overdoing anything. Boredom was not my thing, and I left the castle. I have no idea to where I went next. My guess is back to my bed to await another episode by virtue of the DESIGNED ILLUSIONS.

Retrospect: The top of the building as everywhere else was also cemetery quiet to me. Even the birds that flew overhead and the one caught and in distress didn't make a sound. Many years down the road, my American born sister vacationed in Vasto. She told me the building that I was often seen by the townspeople entering was an old castle.

Otherwise, I would never have known it to be an old castle. Sis said that townspeople could see me, but I couldn't see them. Was it that way my entire time in Vasto and again aboard the "Ship" to America? Was everything normal, but me? I now believe that to be the case. The exceptions being only those made visible to me, as *"Designed Illusions"* by virtue of a Power not of this earth.

CHAPTER 6
The Puddle:
Sometime 1945

I couldn't stay away. I returned to the castle to watch more "birding". there was only one "birdman" there. He still made no acknowledgement of my presence, not even a glance my way. He wasn't having any luck with the birds and still no more birds were to be seen. Maybe there were birds, but everything else, it just wasn't "scripted" for me to see them again.

I walked over to the side of the castle that faced the sea. I was taken by the view. I could take in some of my town from a great vantage point, but still seeing complete emptiness everywhere was wearing on me.

As I was about to leave the castle for good, I could see water coming out of the castle's wall. what I should have seen sooner. Had it just appeared? It seemed the water had accumulated to an enticing stream below and it seemed to flow some distance from the castle grounds.

I eagerly rushed down as fast as my little legs could go to meet up with the stream. I thought of doing a little frolicking in it. The beach of the Adriatic Sea was only a block away. I still had no desire to go there, the reason being that I still couldn't hear the sea nor get a whiff of its pungent salty air. Probably the necessary elements to entice any kid my age or, it just wasn't the right time. On the other hand, I rushed down to meet up with an insignificant amount of water in comparison.

When I got to the area of the rupture in the castle's wall, there was no water and no break in the castle of any kind. Searching the entire perimeter of the castle didn't produce a drop of water. I was becoming suspicious of more illusions that came my way. Enough is enough I thought. I was on my way out of the castle grounds when I saw shrubs that I hadn't seen before. Looking around the shrubs would complete my search, but I didn't expect to find water.

There, it was water, but only a small puddle. I knew immediately it wasn't an ordinary puddle. The water was crystal clear, sparkling and had ripples like a flowing stream. It beckoned me to get on my knees and slurp it. It tasted incredibly delicious. I knew it as an exceptional taste although I couldn't compare it with anything else. I was never thirsty and still hadn't taken in any liquid. It was my first intake of "water.

Slurping the water, I sensed residue water had surrounded my face. Using my hand to wipe it off, I was taken aback that my face and arm were dry. I was finally convinced that illusions were taking place in my life. Undaunted, I slurped twice more, and my face remained dry. I was convinced that the "puddle" was for me and me alone.

The incredible taste of the "water" was what would entice me to return. Maybe the next day is when I return to repeat it all. The "water" was again still delicious, the only reason to return.

The third time was not a charm. The "puddle" was no longer there. I didn't have to look very hard to know where the "puddle" once was, it was then dry, as the rest of the landscape. I left the castle grounds never to return. All via designed humor?

Retrospect: I was then convinced that illusions were becoming common. I didn't know why or how, but I was concerned. I would have no intake of food or drink other than mom's five sugar balls and the puddle water," nor did food or drink ever enter my thoughts at any time. I had no human frailties, a great way to live.

CHAPTER 7
Escape to the Farm: Sometime 1945

My next remembrance was standing in my room with my ear nearly pressed to the wall. I was listening to the aggravating pitch of an air raid siren. I had an idea that it wasn't a good thing. I claim that I had never heard any common noises before but was able to hear an air raid siren.

Mom came rushing in my room from the opening in the partition. It was only the third time at seeing her. The first time as she lay on the opposite side of my bed, the second time since she confronted me with the tray slung on my shoulders. She came in and had a message for me, "We're going to the farm, "we will be safer there!" I had no say about it. No one else in the household would go with us. We immediately left for the farm, leaving by my bedroom door to outside.

I gave some thought to the fact that I was dressed differently for the farm. I wasn't wearing my usual walking shorts and short sleeve shirt, for slacks and a lightweight jacket. I don't ever remember putting on my own clothes or taking them off. Why don't I remember who dressed me? It could be that my slumbers were so severe that I couldn't awaken to do it myself. Shoes, I don't ever remember putting on shoes, wearing shoes or, feeling shoes on my feet. I do know that I never felt anything under my feet, barefoot or not. Being poor, she wouldn't buy shoes for me that I would outgrow without wearing them. She wouldn't know when I would permanently awaken or, if I ever would. Maybe she did get a pair that she had put on me. The shoes probably were from her brother at my age. I just didn't know at that point. I'm sure she wanted me to be properly dressed for the farm where she might have hoped to hobnob with the owners whom she might have known. I just don't remember purposely looking down at my feet for shoes. After all, I would always be comfortable, shoes or not, clothes or not, all by virtue of the Designed Illusions.

The walk wasn't memorable. There was still nothing or anyone for me to see along the way. Then, we came upon a hill. We had to negotiate it downward. Mom said, "I'll go first!" She immediately lost her balance and rolled all the way down. It seemed that she dropped a little paper bag, probably provisions for herself. She wasn't hurt, but might have been embarrassed, and upset. My smile didn't help.

She picked herself up, brushed herself off and continued with the walk. I was still at the top of the hill as she continued to get further away. I learned from her and carefully slid down. Sliding down I couldn't help but look at my feet. It seems I had worn shoes.

I continued to lose sight of her, as I had to pick up my pace. When I turned a corner, she was at the farm's entrance. A man came over to meet us. He pointed and told mom that we were to stay in the barn. She gave him a look of disappointment which said she expected to stay in the farmhouse. She was probably sorry for going there.

In the barn there seemed to me to be four or five others. There was no comradeship between themselves and no welcome for us. They all stood erect and no movement as in "zombies" and no talking between themselves. Was it normal that they would be so callous as not to offer a little word of encouragement to me, regardless of my situation. Being in the barn was boring to me.

I gave the "zombies" no more thought. My interest then was in the farm and my need to venture out. I didn't want to ask mom for permission. She hadn't talked to me since we left the house. I suspected it went much deeper. Was it due to my "coma's" the many sleep cycles, or my inability to dress myself? Maybe all of them, but mostly she must have missed dad terribly. She couldn't figure me out, not eating, not drinking and sleeping a lot. Any which made it more difficult for her to accept me. Then, I never got a hug, kiss or even a good word from her. She may have touched me only when putting clothes on me. I didn't miss, desire, or even think of human physical contact or needs. Of course, it was never tried, so how was I to know what I had missed?

Wanting desperately to leave the confines of the barn and venture into the farm, I didn't want her to turn me down. I walked behind her then quickly outside. The farm was all barren. It could have been due to the war that farmers were reluctant to raise crops that could be confiscated by the warring nations. There were still no odors available to me.

Mom probably didn't think it all out. I'm certain that food was at most scarce and being in a "coma" state meant that I never needed medical attention that they couldn't afford. I cost the family nothing. The clothes that I wore were probably hand-me-downs from her 2 brothers. The poor saved everything. It would turn out that it was my uncle that hated me and wanted me out of the way for being the son of the traitor that chose to leave Italy and fight for the opposition.

Retrospect: Maybe my "coma/deep sleeps" had weighed heavily on mom. She proved that she was controlling. She never once asked me of my opinion about anything. It could also have been my unresponsiveness to her when "asleep" that was difficult for her to accept. I don't want to lose sight of purpose: It could also have led to the thought that without me around she and dad could start over. Then, because of war, they had been separated 4 years.

The complete takeover of me as a young boy was of a spiritual being or, as mom may have thought, Satan.

Years later, Mom told me that Vasto, Italy was a hot bed for paranormal activities. I didn't ask her to elaborate. Maybe, she was trying to coax remembrance from me by making small talk. I didn't want to dredge up the past with her. It was still of that day on the beach which would mentally, permanently separate us, forever. Mom probably knew it, but never brought it up with me. I never made it a secret to be free of her.

CHAPTER 8
Aerial "Dogfight": Sometime 1945

As I walked away from the barn, I thought it best to stay in line with the open door, as it would allow mom to see me all the time.

As I walked on, something of interest caught my attention in an earthen culvert. I left mom's line of sight to check it out. In the culvert was a substance that was not part of the earth. I plucked out a handful and then quickly returned to mom's "line of sight."

The stuff was grayish, smooth and didn't smell bad. It was clay and my first toy. I was able to smell it. Was the sense of smell available to me only for that purpose? It was an odor made available for a reason if I was able to smell, then I should have had memories of other odors that would be memorable. I walked on, shaped the clay into what I wanted, destroyed it, then started over.

No sooner that I bored with the clay machine gun fire entered my hearing. I turned around to look, loud roar of engines entered my hearing. A black plane then came up and by me trailing smoke. Looking up was a gray fighter plane with a star on the fuselage and the winner of the "dogfight".

I couldn't tell the nationality of the first plane, but it appeared to be black in color. The other plane was gray, and it reminds me as an American plane. It then banged to the right and quickly left the scene.

Fearing for my own safety, I anxiously looked for some cover. Close-by was an earthen mound framed with shrubs. I don't remember seeing it before then, but I quickly entered it. A perfect fit and felt "lucky" to have it available to me. I returned to the action. Looking through the spaces in the shrubs, the first plane was still trailing smoke and clearly going down. I feared for the pilot who would soon die when it plowed into the ground..

Then, un-expectantly I saw a fully deployed white parachute. It was a relief to see that the pilot would survive though it bothered me that I didn't see the "pilot" leave the plane. More illusions entered my thoughts. Looking at the parachute that was much further from the doomed plane than is should have been, and I clearly didn't see anyone dangling from the parachute.

As the fighter plane was impacting the barren farmland, it simply disappeared. Then, I quickly turned to focus at the still fully deployed and pilotless "parachute" that soon would touch down. Following it all the way down, it too just vanished. Both "plane" and "parachute" simply disappeared.

My thoughts were certain of more *Illusions*. I looked around the farm for additional witnesses but saw no one else. I was again "bewitched, bothered and bewildered. Leaving the shrub-covered mound, I started back for the barn and no doubt to an angry mom.

She met me about halfway. "It's over, we're going back home!" she gruffly said, then added, "You put yourself in danger!" It would have been futile talking to her my sightings and concerns. I would never take it up with her any of my concerns that were illusions. Then, I wouldn't know how to explain it anyway.

Looking toward the barn and the people there then, I saw them single file walking out of the farm but using a different exit than us. My immediate thought was that no one seemed to be together. Then, a cute and neatly dressed girl, with long black hair, about my age, seemed to be last out of the barn, staring at me as she walked on. She seemed to be alone, following no one. I thought, how sad being alone at such an event. The girl continued to stare at me as she walked on. Why is she staring at me. Did she expect me to stay in the barn with her, just to keep her company? I was getting a little annoyed that I knew nothing of her, but somehow making me feel responsible. I broke off the staring, as she walked on. Could it have been a message of inspiration, I certainly could have used it for myself. Mom and I soon came to our exit of the barn. I had to give the little girl another look, but she and all the others were no longer in my sight. The exception being a single flash image of a man that quickly disappeared at the crest of the hill, as if I needed more Illusions. I never saw the little girl again.

Maybe, those in the barn or even the girl were real, or just as likely more illusions for me. I'll stay with the latter.

Then, I didn't know the name of our town. I didn't know or even cared, until I had to do this report.

At our exit, the same farmhand was there to make certain we were out of the farm.

Retrospect: Then, I was able to hear additional sounds: The "airplane motors" and "machine gun fire." Other than smelling the clay, I was still denied any other smell. The airplane's engine "exhaust", "smoke" from the burning airplane, "machine gun smoke," the odors of the farm and always the odors of my town, still not there for me. Mom was an Italian woman, but she and I still conversed in the English language. As we would with all others. Again, I can only guess as to how. Did she speak to me in Italian, then somehow it got translated into English, when I spoke, it was always in English, when she heard me; was it then translated into Italian, via mental telepathy? Or, as I now know, we were given the ability to speak verbal fluid English. As I have said, any others that I came contact with in Vasto, and then, on the "ship" to America were illusions. I consider it all virtue of the Power Not of Earth. I never took up anything with mom,

CHAPTER 9
Return to "Dodge": Sometime 1945

On the way back to the house, I had difficulty keeping up. We took a different way to avoid the hill that we would've had to climb up.

My aching knee wouldn't allow me to walk any farther. I told Mom, "I can't keep going!" She ignored me and continued with the walk. I got almost in front of her and told her, "If you want me to keep going you will have to carry me!" She wasn't very big, but neither was I. She picked me up, took one step then dropped me. I had laid on the ground with my knee more painful. I looked in horror as mom was getting farther away from me. I didn't know my way back. Mom was at a house that I didn't recognize, Same house but the front door that I never saw. She never looked back at me.

She was clearly angry with me, but she always seemed angry with me. I must have displeased her very much.

I was still face down seeing mom entering the house. What happened to me then?

I don't know. Nothing of remembrance since laying on the ground with severe knee pain.

My guess is that DIVINE POWER took my physical being to put me somewhere. I would never know where. Then, set me somewhere else for another episode.

Retrospect: I still had not eaten nor had any desire for food. Apparently, my life was not mine. I had never complained to anyone about anything and didn't need to until the incident of walking back from the farm. Anyway, there was no one that I could depend on to hear any of my problems. I had an arthritic painful knee, forever. but it had never or since manifested as serious as it did on that day. The pain was the first and only time that I experienced problems with my knee, before then I hadn't experienced any pain or any discomfort. Then, it seems the severe pain came suddenly and with purpose, the purpose could have easily been a message. In my adult years, I would be plagued with the arthritic right knee, but never the debilitating kind that I experienced on that day with mom. The bothersome knee would loom in my distant future that would interfere with my choice of employment. I have only suspicions as to why it manifested as violently as it had in that time and place. Afterward, I wouldn't experience knee pain again of any severity, until much later in life. I had proclaimed that I had never experienced the slightest injury or discomfort of any kind, and then suddenly I had severe knee pain. How do I explain it? I will explain it only as DIVINE purpose that I couldn't depend on my mother, or anyone else in my life. Prophetically, it seems it turned out that way. Looking deeper into it might have been set- up for me to always be remindful of DIVINE POWER.

CHAPTER 10
Publishing the Envelope: Sometime 1945

I was angry with mom for leaving me to fend for myself. Anything I did to displease her, she most likely thought that it was done on purpose. I was tired of her and the illusions. Perhaps I should have appreciated that I didn't need any of my natural senses or requirements to survive. I was never sick or injured, even of minor discomfort except for sudden knee pain. Not to mention being a vibrant and healthy kid without the need of food or drink, and never had to stop for a bathroom break. Thing unknown to me.

As usual, mom was not around when I needed to go out. It might have displeased her again, but I didn't care. Once out, I foresaw another problem. I didn't know where to venture next. I had seen a lot of the town and proceeded toward maybe a town square. I still hadn't seen anyone or anything of interest, nor heard anything or smelled the odors of the town. The lack of normal senses continued to be the way for me. I had to depend on *Designed Illusions*. I didn't know any better.

I was perplexed to see a narrow side street that I don't remember seeing before. Reluctantly, I would "explore" it. Not far into the narrow street, I saw the front of a motorcycle quickly coming my way. I wasn't prepared for I was still in an angry mode. Planned or not, I lightly pushed at the cyclist as he came by me. He quickly stopped and justifiably turned his head to give me a hard look. I gave him a smile as I continued with my walk and with an impromptu limp. The cyclist turned his head and left. I continued with the limp all the way back to my bedroom.

Mom was there when I arrived. She had an unexpected smile for me. Inside, I continued with the limp. "What happened to you?" she wanted to know. I was in no mood to talk to her and just shrugged my shoulders. Maybe, I didn't want to use up my "English speaking minutes?" with her. "Get on the bed!" she ordered. While on the bed I stared at her, and when she turned to me, I had a smirk on my face. Seeing it and with anger, she rushed back to her side of the partition. I thought of another pay back was in store for me. Then, most likely, I went into a sleep cycle until another episode presented itself.

Retrospect: Was the little street that I ventured into always there? When I saw the motorcycle approaching me and when he stopped, I didn't get to hear the rumbling noise that an old type motorcycle would have made. Nor, the smell of the pungent odors of the exhaust fumes. I now suspect it too be illusions and the purpose being, to behave myself? I don't know why, except as all other, another DIVINE purpose.

CHAPTER 11
Last straw:
Sometime 1945

I was asleep on my bed when Mom came rushing into my room. She was yelling at me at the same time waving a pair of shorts at me. She angrily told me, "Y0u get off the bed, get off the bed!" I thought It was because of the antics with the limping and smile at her. The smile that she perceived as more insults at her. The accumulation of years of frustration with my father gone that was taking the toll on her.

Mom ordered me to, "Put these on, they're your swimming trunks, I cut them off an old pair of pants!" I didn't know whose old pair of pants she had them off. I quickly changed into them right in front of her. I shouldn't have been, but I was surprised that they fit me perfectly; as did anything else, I wore. It was probably the only time that I awakened in the sound of her voice; therefore, since I was awake, there was no reason that I couldn't change into the shorts myself. It was the only time that I can remember putting on any of my own clothing then. Maybe I looked forward to the experience. Maybe the pants were once my father's when he was young. More likely one of her brothers. The poor then saved everything.

Mom seemed to have gotten a little control over her rage. She told me, "We're going to the beach!" I wasn't happy going to the beach, especially with her attitude. I didn't know what I would do there. I didn't suspect that I would be going into the water. Swimming never entered my thoughts. Mom knew I couldn't swim. I thought that going to the beach was for her enjoyment only.

We were quickly near the water's edge. I remember nothing of the walk there At the beach she had taken hold of my left hand as if dragging me along. I couldn't feel anything being pulled. As far as I could see, we were alone, and everything was still cemetery quiet for me. The reality, I should have seen ships, the sound of ships, hearing and smelling the sea and seeing people, animals or a vehicle. At least some of the town's activities. I would experience none of those. I could then see to my right the old castle up the hill that was the site of my incredible illusions, but no one at the top. Walking along, I thought that it was strange that we kept walking although we could stop anywhere, since everywhere along the shoreline looked the same to me. After the long walk I then see someone coming toward us. He appeared to be in his late 20's, and of all things, he was carrying a bundle of straw. As he began to get closer, I could see that the bundle of straw was tied around with twine. I expected him to pass by us.

Instead, he stopped just in front of us. Looking only at me, he asked the stupid question, "Would you like to ride on it.' "He put the bundle in the water The bundle of straw was the raft for me.. I had a quick **no** for him.

The young man then looked at mom as if for assistance. She looked away from us. I began to think that she was part of it. I had a terrible feeling.

He then motioned the bundle of straw toward the sea as he again asked me, "would you like to get on my raft." Then, I got angry and again told him. "NO!" Mom then piped in, "Get on, get on, it's all right!" I couldn't agree with her less, but I wanted to be obedient.

The man waited for me in the water with the bundle of straw bobbing near him. I waded out to the bundle of straw. The water was deeper than it looked. it took a second try for me to hop on. It quickly began to break apart. I tried to find the safest spot, but there wasn't one. My only choice was to stay perfectly still. Maybe that way it would take a little longer to drown. I didn't know what else to do.

I felt the bundle of hay being pulled farther out to sea. I then looked toward the beach at mom. She was still in her dress looking away from it all. I called out to her, "bring me in!" She totally ignored me. I then looked at the man as he struggled swimming and pull on the bundle at the same time, No doubt try for deeper water. I again looked toward the beach at mom, still with her back to me. With genuine anger, I called out to her, again: "BRING ME IN, NOW!" I was surprised that she relented. She turned her head and waved to the man and without reluctance; he pulled the remainder of the bundle of straw and me back to shore. I immediately rolled off it. The man picked up the remnant straw and left the beach as quickly as he came. I looked at Mom with anger as she still looked away from me. I left her sitting on the grassy part of the beach. I wouldn't see the man again. I walked away without memory of getting back to my bedroom? changing into my walking shorts? or what I did next? I can now only surmise that DIVNE POWER stepped in again for me and put me somewhere, again.

The thought that all may have been *Scripted.*

Retrospect: I don't remember having the feeling of wetness while on "the bundle of or sand on me when leaving the water. I surely must have been barefoot walking away from the beach on the town's decrepit street but feeling no discomfort. All conversations were in English including the young Italian man; I don't believe he was an illusion. Now, I believe that my uncle hired the guy. Only uncle would know and associate himself with the young man and of course mom being involved. Apparently, I could also yell out the English language. I would always struggle with the possibility that mom wanted to off me. If so, she had to have more help. That help was her grandmother, the only other person in the home. It would be years in the future to know my uncle and that he was the architect of the beach fiasco. I learned in America years later that he was my uncle when mom told me simply, "your uncle in Italy died." It was mom's complacent about her that told me don't bother with any condolence. I wasn't about to offer any.

CHAPTER 12
Enemy within: Sometime 1945

I have nothing to report after the beach fiasco. Until I was asleep when startled awake by a stranger who had burst into my room. He didn't give me a glance as he brought in a large tray of fish, then placed the tray on a little table.

He just stood there until mom came from behind the partition to meet-up with him. All she said to him was, "Leave a fish for him, he needs to eat, he doesn't eat!" The stranger had an answer for mom, but I couldn't hear it. Mom angrily left to return to the main part of the house. The fisherman picked up his tray of fish and left as he came, probably headed for the market to sell his fish. I must have then returned to another sleep cycle. Gratefully, there was no fish for me. Sadly, from then on, I would know him as being part of my life.

Retrospect: I couldn't smell anything that had to do with fish. It would be many years before finding out the identity of the fisherman. He was mom's brother, my uncle. and the "mastermind" of the beach fiasco. Mom seemed to try to make some amends for her part but getting a fish for me was not the way. I still had no desire for any food. The reason for not being able to smell odors. To have the natural sense of smell would negate my lack of desire for food. It was the first time ever seeing my uncle, although we lived under the same roof for over 7 years. I still hadn't seen my grandmother since she had then stared at me with a frown as she stood at the end of my bed. Grandmother, uncle and maybe mom believed that since I was surviving without food or drink, then Satan must have possessed me. Or, just as likely they thought I was just being stubborn. That made it easy for them to disrespect me. Vasto, Italy was then a hotbed of paranormal sightings as mom once told me. Real or imagined, as mom needed to tell me years later, as though she would grow suspicious and eventually became convinced that I too was the product of paranormal via the Divine power. My thought now is that it took her long enough. What made mom finally come to that conclusion? Could it be that by her own admission, that I hadn't had anything to eat or drink not counting the puddle water my entire time in Vasto, and beyond.

CHAPTER 13
My Paper Plane Maker: Sometime 1945

I don't know if anything happened between seeing the fisherman/uncle who had come into my room and awakened me. Then, again awaken to an overwhelming need to venture somewhere. Then, maybe the fall season, closing in on winter. I still wore the same shorts and the short sleeve shirt and comfortable. No doubt barefoot.

I quickly went out and just stood in the middle of the alleyway. I looked toward the town square trying to determine where I needed to venture next. The decision was made easier for me when I heard: "Pasquale!" It was the first time that I heard my name. I turned to see a boy a year or so older than me. I remembered seeing him twice before. He would wave to me as if he knew me. I don't remember if I waved back. I think he lived in a house somewhere nearby, but as I turned to leave toward the town square, he yelled to me again, "Come here, I want to show you something!"

The boy stood trans-fixed on me with a ready sheet of paper at his side. I had no reluctance being with him, since I hadn't decided where to venture next anyway. He said, "I want to show you how to make a paper airplane!" He then went to a flat surface on the ground and began folding the piece of paper. He was quick to finish it.

He proudly showed it to me. It was then a standard looking dart-like airplane. He "launched" it, but it didn't fly well or far. I stood there watching him try for better results. I was just trying to be a good neighbor. The kid didn't appear to give me another thought as he continued to try and fly his un-cooperative airplane. I left him there and again gave thought of my next venture. I was getting frustrated that nothing was coming to mind. I just knew that I needed to go somewhere.

Beginning the walk to the town square, I was abruptly stopped again, then by my fisherman/uncle. It was the first time that I heard him speak. With a gruff attitude, he told me, "We need firewood, go get some!" Without another word or instructions, he quickly returned indoors via the main door. I stood parallel to my room's still open door. I don't remember using the door to exit my room. I do say that I knew more than my years of any situation would have allowed. I knew what uncle meant by firewood, but I had never seen a fire log or one burning before. My bedroom door was still open. I don't know why it was open. I could then see a large fire log burning nicely in my fireplace. I was again perplexed, and my immediate thought was that this was another illusion. Another reason being that only a few minutes earlier, I had left my room and there was no burning log. Could uncle have ignited that hard-to-come-by log for me or anyone else in the house se.in no chance of that, I thought. He wouldn't have wasted a log fire on me or anyone else.

I didn't need heat. Last winter I was perfectly comfortable without a log fire. I couldn't make any sense of that log fire, but it gave me the sense of purpose that I needed for the next venture, firewood for the fisherman/uncle. I would try to please him.

Did I know that I would need tools to come up with fire logs successfully? Probably not, but at my age I wouldn't have been able to use them anyway. Was there a sinister reason why uncle would send me to get the firewood, without additional instructions? I knew then, without a doubt, that uncle didn't like me. It would be many years before I knew that he was an uncle and that hated me. In the future when mom looked at me and told me her brother had died. I started to console her a little, but she abruptly stopped me and walked away.

Uncle didn't tell me where I needed to go for his firewood, but I remembered the "scooter boy" pointing to the forest. Without the "scooter boy," I wouldn't know of the forest. I would have passed up on the "crashed airplane" if I should have happened upon it. In no time I was in the forest. It was quiet and desolate even without a tweet of a bird. I had become accustomed to total emptiness and silence everywhere, but not even seeing or the tweet of a bird. Even uncle didn't seem too bad. It was all creeping on me, being alone. I continued with the search for uncle's firewood. There wasn't a single branch on the ground to be seen. As I walked on, I was convinced that I would find firewood, somewhere.

I then saw low treetops just ahead and it revealed to me that I would soon come upon a hillside. There I was convinced that I would find the firewood and continued to look for firewood as I walked on.

I then saw a figure of a man just stood looking at me. He seemed to be in early thirties, nice looking. He was dressed, I can only say, futuristic. Dressed either in all white or light grey. His pullover was up to his neck, without pockets, buttons or zippers. He then asked if he could make a paper airplane for me. Thought of my neighbor kid and his attempt at a paper airplane. I expected the same, but I said sure, but I continued the search for the fisherman/uncle's firewood.

In short order I was at tall trees. I didn't expect to be looking down at a very long and steep hillside. I could see many branches that I would gather for the fisherman/uncle.

As I was about to take a first step downward for tree branches a familiar voice said to me: "Here!" In front of my eyes was a most beautiful technical thing still called a paper airplane, it also had four paper engines each with four propellers.

As I looked around for the submitter of my great prize I saw the futuristic man at the same place as before, his back to me walking away. I wouldn't see him ever again.

I thought about flight. I thought that it either would fly well for my greater acceptance, or that it wouldn't fly at all. I was convinced of the latter. I thought the main cause would be the four little paper propellers that would cause "wind drag." Of course, wind drag was a relatively new term.

Had I "just happened" to be standing at part of the hill that was free of trees and other obstructions for the flight, all the way to the bottom?

I was pessimistic of any good result when I "launched." I expected it to immediately end at my feet. I "launched" it and as if a gust of wind took the plane to the height of about six feet.

In flight the plane didn't waver left or right at all and continued on the same exact trajectory heading for the bottom. I was momentary mesmerized by its perfect flight, but I anxiously wanted it to end its flight before it reached the part of the hill where I couldn't retrieve it. I could see that my desperation was in vain, as it continued in its perfect flight all the way to the very bottom. As if by command, it dipped its nose for a perfect landing. It was the end of the perfect flight and the end of the perfect paper airplane. I was aghast at losing my gift.

However, I had to proceed with the reason I was there, to collect firewood for uncle. Maybe, the only reason for being there was to receive my gift. I went down the hillside only as far as I dared and collected the largest branches that I could get too. When I had enough, I sadly looked for the last time at my paper airplane visible at the bottom of the hill. Then, as an epiphany, the airplane did exactly what it was supposed to do, fly well. It flew as perfectly as any paper airplane could. Otherwise, it was still only a piece of paper. I couldn't take it with me and carry the tree branches back home.

I picked up branches and headed home. I stopped to give my gift a final look. I couldn't see it, because it wasn't there anymore.

There I was, certain where I was, certain uncle waited anxiously for my return. As I walked on, I continued to lose branches. When I reached the house, I had dropped all but a few.

Uncle was there to meet me. He could see me arriving from a window in the main part of the house. (I still hadn't been to the main part of the house and never would, nor had ever been invited there). He shouted at me, "That isn't firewood!" then quickly returned inside. I dropped the remaining few and returned inside, I think. I never have any remembrance of me ever opening or closing any door! Once inside I wouldn't go further than my bedroom. I wasn't tired, but I probably would occupy my bed until another episode presented itself. I could see that the fireplace once had burning logs. Then, the fireplace was again cold and clean. It didn't bother me that I was still convinced that all are just *Illusions*.

Retrospect: What was the purpose of it all? I was given the ability to survive birth and be robust without any normal earthly necessities. Besides the many illusions in my past and others yet to come, was physical *Entity* the necessary element that came forward to somewhat ease my fears? The *Entity* and I of course "conversed" in English. I would not see the *entity* again. Maybe he, being not very far from me in spirit being my guardian angel and to survive my uncle was what I needed most?

When an American born sister visited Vasto she had mentioned to me of a boy that asked about me and that we were friends. She told me his name that I don't remember or never knew it before. Could the boy have been the neighbor kid with his uncooperative paper airplane? I only know of that one brief "playtime" with him. What was his role, if any, in the equation? Was the kid a real person that was spiritually pulled into the *"script"* without his knowledge, but for what purpose? All possible only by
DIVINE POWER

CHAPTER 14
The Fireplace:
Sometime 1945

Light awakened me up again. Then, it was coming from a medium size burning log in the fireplace. It looked to be a replica of the log that burned there prior to my going into the forest. Just like the first "fire log," I considered it as another illusion for me.

Nevertheless, I got off the bed to get a closer look. I had never seen a "burning log" close-up before. I had nothing in the room to keep me occupied. Illusion or not, I pulled up the stool and sat closer to the fireplace just to enjoy watching the perfect "burning log." I had no idea that being close to a fire would at least be more uncomfortable. I expected heat from it.

Almost immediately, I saw something close to the "fire," next to the fireplace wall. It appeared to be a small circular piece of metal, which seemed to have an image of a bearded man. Again, I thought just another illusion. I got off the stool for a closer look. I desperately wanted it. Since I thought it to be an illusion it wouldn't hurt me. Putting my hand only close to the "medallion," I was "burned." I yelled in pain. I thought how stupid of me for putting my hand in the "fire." I began to reconsider it not being an illusion, after all.

Upon hearing my scream, mom came rushing in from behind the partition. "What happened?" she asked. "I put my hand in the fire to get the thing out!" I tried to explain. She didn't look at the fireplace. Maybe she thought it was just another of my childish antics. She took my hand and looked it over and said, "Wait here!" then went back behind the partition. She soon returned with a white pan, probably a bedpan. She put it down, squatted over it, adjusted her dress and then I heard her pee hitting the pan. She then again asked for my hand. She acted as though she was going to put it in the pan. Happily, she released it. It didn't justify putting my hand in the "ancient antiseptic." My hand was not burned, and I was no longer in pain. Mom still hadn't looked toward the fireplace. Couldn't she see the "burning log?" more of *Designed Illusions?* Was the DIVINE angry at me about something, or just showing off?

I went back to sit at the fireplace again. I just stared at the still nice "burning log." and looked for the "medallion," It was no longer at the fireplace, nore anything that even resembled it. Illusions again entered my thoughts of the "fire log." I would continue to enjoy the still nice burning, but troublesome "fire log." I sat so close to the "burning log" that if it had been a real log fire, I would be forced to move much further back. I couldn't feel the heat. Anyway, I was only interested in looking at the fire.

I didn't know anything about log fire. I didn't know that it requires constant working of the log. That it produces smoky odors and it that it shoots off hot embers, I experienced nothing like that. I certainly thought it to be another false "event," but better than a real log fire. There were no tools, should working the log ever was necessary, all via a humorous Divine Power?

Mom came in my room again, then carrying a bowl. I was then sitting away from the fireplace. I must have become leery of the "burning log." She came next to me and asked, "Can you eat these?" I didn't even look in the bowl, as I shook my head (no). She then lessened her request. "Can you eat just one?" I then nodded (yes). She shelled it for me and I ate it. It was a roasted chestnut. I liked it, but I refused to eat more, much to her dismay and disappointment. It may have been the Christmas season (1945). Chestnuts symbolized the season in Italy. It is difficult for me to blame her for all she had to endure from life and me. It was almost sinful not eating in Italy, besides causing death.

I wouldn't eat another chestnut for many years to come, but I never forgot the taste of that single chestnut. There was nothing else that would entertain my pallet but shook my head (no) when she again asked me to eat more. She returned the bowl to her part of the house. She came and went without ever looking at or commenting on the still nice "burning log."

I still hadn't been invited to the main part of the house and I had no desire to go there. I think it was mostly uncle that didn't want me there, or just as likely all *"scripted"* per the DIVINE. Uncle hated my very existence. He probably didn't think I had a right to live. I believe, after all, that he was the architect of the beach fiasco.

That single chestnut was my only intake of any food of my entire remembrance since awakening sometime in the winter of 1944/45. Not counting the sugar balls Mom concocted for me to sell, about a year prior. I still had no intake of liquid since slurping the "puddle water" at the old castle. Now, as then, I consider the "puddle water" an illusion.

Then, I didn't know that not eating was abnormal. I didn't eat because I didn't desire food and never saw anyone eat, ever. I never had an appetite.

Mom came in my room again but stood near the entrance. She waved an old fashion waffle iron at me, the type with long handles that goes over an open flame. She yelled out to me, "Can I make a waffle for you?" I shook my head (no) or said no. Then, she yelled out her concern, "You got to eat, you don't eat!". She angrily left to return the waffle iron. The fire needed for the waffle was most likely in her part of the house, a real log fire. Mom still didn't get it, blaming me for not eating.

She must have known that uncle didn't want to feed me, a scenario that she seemed to overlook. What if she succeeded in getting me to eat? I would then require more food than she could ever deliver. I would always be hungry, and surely uncle would find a way too off me, with or without anyone's help. I was the son of my father, the man who chose to go to America and fight against Italy and leaving others to care for me,.

although, there was very little caring required of me or, none at all.

I understand mom's frustration with me. Mom wanted me to be a part of her life. It also showed her controlling ways. It would take many years for her to realize that I was not responsible for my life, but at the control of a Power unknown to us, besides that of Satan. I refuse to believe it to be Satan. Mom should have had at least some inkling of abnormality since by her own account: "He never ate in Italy."

I don't know how long the illusionary "burning log" had kept me occupied, before I would have to move on to what would be the next episode?

CHAPTER 15
Announcement: Sometime 1945-46

The next thing that I remember is just standing around, not doing anything noteworthy as mom came rushing into the bedroom. She went directly out into the alleyway, then stood gazing at the Adriatic Sea. She then waved at me to join her there. My immediate thought was that another walk on the beach was in store.

Joining her, she pointed to the beach and told me, "They just pulled a man out of the water. He had crabs all over him!" I strained to see what she was looking at and as usual, I saw only a placid Adriatic Sea, no ships or vessels of any kind and no people, animals or vehicles, nothing, I had no trouble only visualizing crabs on a dead body. I had never seen a dead person or a crab before, to my knowledge. Without another word, she rushed back inside and returned to the main part of the house, leaving me standing in the alleyway. I thought that it was all so weird...again.

At some point, maybe even a few minutes after we spent the "quality time" out in the alleyway, she came back to me with the news, "Soon, we will be going to America. and you will be seeing your father!"

I had a neutral feeling by the news. I had no memory of dad. Mom seemed optimistic, but I couldn't join her there. I couldn't trust her anymore, maybe meeting dad could be a good thing. It didn't ease my deep anxiety about traveling to the unknown and meet dad. Non-the-less, leaving the fisherman/uncle behind would be a good thing.

Not to mention finally leaving more illusions behind, Wishful thinking.

World War2 must have ended for mom to be so optimistic.

I had turned eight years old or about at that time. Knowing then what I know now of uncle, I would've been eager to leave town and take my chances with dad in America. I looked over at the fireplace for a little more comfort, but it was again cold and clean.

I remember nothing since her announcement of our impending trip to America. Maybe, I went into another "sleep cycle" and had awaited another episode to take place. After all, I now consider everything as *"scripted"* via a DIVINE POWER.

CHAPTER 16
Leaving for America: Sometime 1946

My next recall, incredibly, from a short distance away, I looked at myself standing "tall" and saw that I was dressed the same way as I had on our venture to the farm, again wearing trousers and the lightweight jacket. But I focused on the shoes that I wore. The shoes were black and very shiny. The shoes un-expectantly stood out for me.

Standing tall and then as a singular me, I stared down at my feet at the shiny black shoes, without socks, as always, when I wore shoes, I couldn't feel them on me. I don't recall ever being fitted for shoes. They could have fit tight or loose, it didn't matter, as any other time, I couldn't feel them on my feet. Then it was I never felt anything on me for any adjustment.

I don't think I ever wore underwear. The only new addition was the pair of shiny black shoes. I still didn't know anything while standing there. I knew that I was again dressed for travel. The travel to America didn't enter my mind. Looking at the cold and clean fireplace, desiring another burning log to keep me occupied. A few feet away from me I spotted a small suitcase. I knew then it was traveling time, our earthly possessions in that one little suitcase.

I still don't remember dressing myself or putting on shoes. I guess mom was still the one who had to it I must have been unresponsive to awaken and dress myself. She no doubt blamed me, probably as a lazy and uncooperative kid. Now, I blame the DIVINE and all as *"scripted."* The only time that I remember dressing myself was putting on swimming trunks and the beach fiasco. I was then at the upper floor of the house where I had never been. I was standing next to mom when grandma entered. Mom then left my side to be with grandma. They hugged, kissed and cried. .A sad sight indeed. It was only the second time seeing grandma. The other time is when I saw her staring at me at the end of my bed, at my first recall, about a year prior. She had nothing for me. She didn't even look my way. For the first time I felt like persona-non-grata. To be fair, she may have been afraid of her son, my uncle, if she showed any caring for me.

I have absolutely no memory of our trip to the "ship". When leaving the house, the mode of travel, length of travel to the Ship/s Port. Nothing came to mind. My face was very close to the metal of the Ship. I was very angry at missing out on the trip to the Ship. Next recall was mom got my hand for the walk up the ship's gangplank. Mom held firmly to my hand. It wasn't that she feared me leaving her She, had an equilibrium problem due to an enlarged heart and high blood pressure, as she told me years later. We stood waiting for prominent people for the ship. No one came. Then, mom went to the ships railing. She looked down on the dock. I follower there. On the dock was uncle pacing. . Of course, I saw no one else and presumably, was the one who took us to the ship. She was giving him slight bon farewell waves. She wouldn't give up on it as uncle continued to look away from us. I then thumbed my nose at him. I never saw anyone doing that. Uncle turned and looked at her, but not at me. He probably was still around to make certain that she wouldn't change her mind at leaving Italy.

Thankfully, a voice behind us said his message: "You've got to get going" I turned to see a lone crewman, dressed in brownish overalls. Mom then followed him to our cabin. I rushed to be with her as she entered our to be cabin. I didn't see her showing any document or ask of her. For me everything was still cemetery quiet. I don't know what mom experienced. I would never ask her, all because of her part in the beach fiasco, I couldn't forgive her. I didn't think that *Illusions* would follow me once out of Vasto, Italy. Mom would never return to Italy.

Once in our cabin, we immediately sat on our bunks. I fully expected mom to start a lengthy conversation. She didn't feel the necessity to give me the heads-up on our voyage. Unbelievably, I barely knew of her, and it was the only time that we had ever sat together. Other than our trip to the Ship. I'm aware that it was probably the result of being in a "coma" and "deep sleeps" for my first seven years, or, it was just her way. Mom immediately laid down with her face to the wall. That was good for me. But, if anything happened to her while on the trip, I wouldn't have a clue to our destination once we reached America. Maybe she was angry enough with me that she didn't care. Or, as always, she thought that she could handle everything. Mom always had a positive attitude to a fault. At times, it could turn disastrous, thus my need for DIVINE POWER, that I now believe was there for me.

Retrospect: Beside the lone crewman. Then, I wouldn't see or ever would see another crewman or, any other person on the "Ship" *Illusions* would continue to be the way for me.

CHAPTER 17
Ship of Foolery-Food: Sometime 1946

As the ship seemingly began pulling out, mom immediately sat up and heaved. Looking at her I was about to follow suit, but only dry heaved. I would have been very surprised if anything came up since I never ate anything, As I have tried to explain. She lay down and soon had to heave again. Afterward, she went into the restroom for paper towels to clean up after herself. Gratefully, I couldn't smell anything, even the puke. I would never have the need to use the "ship's" restroom. Were my natural senses still at the whim of the DIVINE? I absolutely believe it. I didn't hear the sound of the gangplank being removed.

Then, I wouldn't become seasick. It certainly wouldn't be the same in later years. Mom and I then exchanged roles on the "ship". I would be the one being vigilant, while mom did my old role of deep sleeps. Did it just happen that way or *"Scripted?"*

I was sitting on my bunk when mom awakened. I didn't know the time of day, as neither of us had a timepiece or a calendar. I never knew anything of time, dates and year. I'm hungry, go get me some food!" then she demanded, "Get some food for yourself, you need to eat too, you don't eat!" I told her, "I don't know where to get food!" She became irate, "GO, GO!" she scowled. I would be a dutiful son and try to find food for her. I didn't intend to eat anything. I still had no appetite.

It was still daylight when I went on deck in search of food. I don't remember experiencing darkness or even a rainy day, not a single raindrop ever touched me.

I thought there were others that I could count on while on deck, mostly crewmembers, forever an optimist. As I walked on, I stayed close to the railing heading to the rear of the ship. I wouldn't see a single person. The only good thing was that I was still totally comfortable. That is to say, I still felt nothing. Were my senses still being manipulated?

It was the dead of winter. I couldn't blame anyone for not going on deck. It must have been a very harsh environment, the cold, movement of the ship and the wind blasting away. Of course, I would experience nothing like that. I did expect to see at least the one of the ships crewmen.

If my senses were normal, then I would have had issues with mom for sending me out in such unknowns searching for her food. If I still had to go out, I would be searching for food for my need, as well, if it all were normal.

Without help, I had no idea where I would find food. I don't remember being afraid, just a daunting task ahead of me. While I pondered at the railing near our cabin then noticed a little black object on the wall. It looked as though it was something to talk into. I thought it might be for passengers in distress, like me.

Only as I got close to the object and without me saying a word that a male voice asked: "Can I help you?" I was taken aback. I hadn't touched it. Apparently, I could speak into it without picking it up. I understood him perfectly, as he spoke my language, English, but nothing would come out of my mouth. Then, just to keep the "voice" from ending, I tried gibberish nonsense.

The "voice" seemed irate and replied: "what?" Totally embarrassed, I meekly began to walk away, but turned back around to give the "voice" another try. I didn't want to give up so easily. As I again walked to pick up the object and again only getting close to it that, the "voice" said its message, "We don't deliver food to the cabins, if you want to eat you will have to go to the dining room!" The message and the messenger again had taken me aback. However, it answered my question, without asking it.

Armed with that knowledge, I returned to the cabin and gave Mom the result of my search. Once in the cabin area, it occurred to me that I forgot which one was my cabin's door. Taking a chance on one of the doors, I slightly opened it. Peeking in, I saw a woman laying down facing the wall. Again, I recognized her dress. I would have to remember the cabin number, which I did. I could also read numbers. Maybe, it was #3.

Mom sat up when I entered. I remained standing as I told her about the message, "If you want to eat, we will have to go to the dining room!" I thought she would then give up on food. She replied, "I'm not going to the dining room, but you go there and get food for yourself, then you can bring some back for me!" I didn't expect that answer. She knew that I didn't eat, but I wanted to be a dutiful son.

I went out again to another seemingly daunting task. I had to find the dining room. At least nothing physically bothered me. As I got to mid-ship again, I stopped and looked at the "microphone" and maybe try to get some help from it again. But I didn't want to press my luck, until I had no choice and continued on.

Shortly, I was about the rear of the ship. There was a sign that was in English, "Passengers are not allowed beyond this point!" I could read the sign, I understood numbers, but I had yet to see the name of the ship. Behind the sign was a metal ladder that went straight down to another level which housed a building. My search had ended. I gave serious thought of going back to the little black object on the wall for assistance.

The entire ship was still cemetery quiet, normal for me. Just as the search for the elusive dining room would end, an unusual odor filled my nostrils. Looking around I saw a long black plume of smoke coming from out of the top of a nearby building. My eyes then caught brightness coming out the panes of glass of its double doors.

The odor seemed to be cooking odors, although I had never experienced odors of any kind, other than the smell of "clay" at the farm. Not even odors of the fishing village of Vasto, Italy. Then, I thought that I smelled swordfish. I don't know why swordfish?

I waddled like a duck to the brightness of the doors. I then slid my eyes up a glass pane. I didn't want to be detected for fear of being invited in and offered food. Inside, I could see three people, a woman behind the counter and two men sitting at a dining table. The three seemingly not involved with anything. I found the dining room and mom would know the results of my search. I didn't think they would allow outtake food.

On my way back to the cabin, I stopped abruptly and turned around. I would sit at a bench seat. I felt that I deserved some quality time for myself. The sea was still calm. I never saw anything than a calm sea. The great vastness of where we were was very intimidating. It was all very quiet still, which made it easier to accept. I gave some thought of probable sea tragedies that happened where we were. Then, I thought if I stayed I could see crewman come out of the building below. I waited to be entertained watching swordfish being caught. Luckily, reality quickly set in. The ship was moving too fast for fishing and the swordfish probably were brought on board to be food.

The lack of brightness of light coming through the dining room glass panes I may have thought the day was turning to dusk. Apparently, it was not yet serving time. If I was on a real ship and what I now know of ships, which isn't very much, the building below would probably have been the noisy engine room. Everything still cemetery quiet.

Returning to the cabin, mom was still lying down, facing the wall, in a sleeping position. She wouldn't wake up to quiz me about food. Maybe she came to realize that to eat meant that she would only heave it up. She may have been right. She wouldn't order me to get food for the remainder of the trip. I too lied on my bunk and joined Mom in a much deserve sleep.

Retrospect: If the little black object on the outside wall was a microphone, it would be difficult for someone to use it that didn't know how. To talk, the button needed to be pressed, to hear, it's released. That would have to be repeated throughout the conversation. Again, I heard the messages in English. If it were a real ship, the message would have to be repeated in all languages for the passengers on board. Up to that point, I still hadn't seen anyone else on deck. I thought the cooking odor was swordfish. I had never seen a swordfish, but I could visualize its long bill and all. I had never seen crabs before either. I claim manipulation of all my normal senses and needs. Being able to smell the cooking odors at that specific time and place for the purpose of enabled me to find the "dining room?" Was it all still *"scripted?"* at whim of THE DIVINE POWER?

CHAPTER 18
Ship of Foolery-Liberty: Sometime 1946

I clearly heard the ships intercom message: "We will be docked here for 2 days, you may leave the ship if you want, but you must return when the horn sounds or you will be left behind!" The message didn't preclude, "This is the captain speaking." The speakers weren't ever visible anywhere. The message didn't appear to wake up mom. Her back to me I couldn't tell. Need I say that I heard the message only in English presumably, it was an American ship, I hadn't seen the ship's name anywhere to know. The "Ship" seemingly didn't have other foreign passengers that would require hearing the messages in their respective languages. We were Italians and should have been registered as such. If all were normal.

On the other hand, maybe I should have come to grips that the entire ship and anyone on board except mom and I were of *Designed Illusions*. I hadn't yet seen a single person considered passengers. What about voices? I should at least have heard a voice or two, not of crewmembers. but not a peep anywhere. I don't have to convince myself of extreme abnormalities, I've been convinced of it for a long time.

And, I had yet to see anyone else onboard beside that lone "crewman" and the 3 "people" in the dining room, those were all that I saw. Mom remained comatose. I needed to check out the message. I was quickly on the deck. I wanted to see additional passengers board or leave. Forever an optimist. At the railing, I looked all around, but not a single person to be seen. Then, I spotted something of interest to me then barely 8 years old. It was a wire compound and close-by. I could see that the gate was left partially open. It was daytime. I wouldn't ever hear the huge gangplank being put in place that could be very noisy. Nor the ship's horn that never sounded.

I was quickly down on the dock and quickly at the compound's open gate. I could see inside the entire compound but, wouldn't venture very far inside. It was not what I expected. It was empty of men and materials, with exception of many bullets that littered the dirt. I thought they were of attractive brass, copper and shiny. I would take 4 with me.

As I was about to leave, I realized that I could be stopped for stealing. Maybe I would then see another person holding me back at the most inopportune time and would miss my union with dad. I threw the bullets back in the dirt.

Going back to the ship, it was no surprise that I still saw no one, but for the first time the name of the ship came into view. I stood transfixed at the ship's huge acute angled silvery bow, and the name of the ship. At the very top in bold letters was the name: "BROWN." Only the last name was clearly visible. I could see the first words of its name, but they were being blurred. Still, no one to be seen. Can anyone imagine not seeing anyone or hearing anything and know it as abnormal.

I was surprised to see Mom sitting up when I got back. She was waiting for me. "I want to get off the ship too!" She insisted. She must have seen my look of concern, and then added, "I've been here before. I was relieved to hear it. She didn't tell me where we are and I didn't ask. It could very well have been Naples, Italy, or wherever.

My next remembrance, in the town we were in the throng of many townspeople waiting for something to happen. I didn't know what? I saw someone using a long stick to apply grease to an already cleared and erected to about a 25-foot utility pole. There was applause upon seeing a couple of men as they appeared dressed only in shorts. The pole had many prizes strung at different places and levels, on the pole. The better prizes, money were strung at the very top on a cross-arm. Someone with the stick/mop finished applying grease to the pole.

The objective of the game was simply for the participants, all men wearing only shorts, one at a time to shimmy up the pole, grab whatever they could before the inevitable, sliding back down. There was always someone there eager to re-apply more grease as needed for the next participant.

The game was very comical and entertaining. It allowed mom and me to share a laugh. Sadly, it would be the last laugh we would ever share. I saw only two minor successes before we left. I would have liked to have stayed longer, but mom wanted to move on. She never asked what I wanted. We soon came upon a building that was a movie theater. She wanted to take in a movie. It was probably her intention all along. It would be my first movie.

The movie's genre was romantic, and I was very bored by it. This, 8 years old wasn't interested in romance. I never experienced any kind of affection, even as a family unit, until witnessing mom and grandma hugging and kissing before we left Vasto.

The genre suddenly changed. The ending: (An old man wearing a suit was walking along in his bomb out town. He used his cane to help himself maneuver through the rubble. He noticed something of interest to him. Walking to it, he saw that it was a large piece of metal protruding through some of the rubble. He decided to poke at it with his cane. There was a great explosion. The old man had set off an unexploded bomb. Mom gasped, I thought wow good movie (In black and white). Why did the movie change from romance to violence so abruptly, was pity taken on me and I was allowed a little entertainment? Probably not, but just a thought.

Once outside the theater, she could have gotten some much-needed food for herself that must have been available I suppose at many eateries. Instead, she bought a little piece of something to eat while walking back to the ship. She pointed it at me as if to offer me part of it. I just shook my head (no). I wasn't interested in food and drink. We were walking back toward the dock when the rear of our "ship" came into view. I looked directly at the back of the "ship" that should have had its name displayed, but there was no name. Then, I didn't think too much of it. A real ship of that size would have its name prominently displayed on the rear, I thought.

Retrospect: For many years, I thought of the wire compound and its purpose: 1st that it was a pistol firing range because the bullets were .45 cal. How did I know that? Maybe it was seeing war movies in my later years. Then, the compound was a prisoner holding place. Finally, most likely, it was an abandoned American ammunition depot. Bullets had dropped out of a broken case. Although being around many "people" at the local custom's (pole) game, then walking to and in the theater, for me to say that it was all normal, I would have to experience something memorable to fully believe it. Such as the odors of the town, yelling close to me, vendors being aggressive with us, money being exchanged in the theater, anything negative. There was no such thing, and it wasn't because all Naples or wherever residents were known for their civility.

At the same time. I don't want to discredit anything that was all or partially normal. Non-the-less, all is still the report of ILLUSIONS. Walking past the rear of the "BROWN" is the last that I recall of that episode as we re-entered the "SHIP".

I would come to believe that everything with mom, the town and all was the DIVINE POWER giving me a break. I enjoyed it all for a change.

CHAPTER 19
Ship of Foolery-shots: Sometime 1946

The ship's intercom came to life again. The new message was ominous: "Everyone is to come on deck for their immunization/vaccination shot". "You, can't leave the ship without it!" I looked all around for the speaker. It's worthy to note that the message still didn't include, "This is the captain speaking."

I heard every word but wished I hadn't. I was totally freaked out as never before. I had only one definition in my English vocabulary for the word "shot." The message hadn't moved mom at all. I wouldn't alert her the message might have been a mistake. I didn't want to leave the comfort of my bunk to be "shot" either. Finally, there was a woman last in a very short line of women. She was completely visible to me while the others were greyish, silent and stationary. I believed the woman just ahead of me but not any other of the women. Suddenly, a young boy about my age positioned himself just behind me. I had to ask him: "What is a "shot"? He replied in English: "They will put a needle in your arm, but it won't hurt, I have gotten it before, watch, he said! The boy then broke from standing behind me toward a lone man wearing a brown suit at the end of the room, with a long needle. The boy had his arm fully extended to receive the "shot".

He got no grief from anyone for his bold move. Without asking the "boy" anything, the man quickly gave the boy his "shot." More incredibly, the boy then let out a blood-curling scream and with the same sprinter speed, quickly ran by me and out of sight, still screaming. The "man" with the syringe walked back from where he came. It freaked me out.

I thought my hero kid was a dud. I too with good speed of my own quickly returned to my cabin and my bunk. Mom still "comatose," was no wiser to all the happenings. I curled up on my bunk and vowed that I wouldn't go back on deck. If I were to get a "shot," then they would have to come in my cabin and do the deed there.

Mom and I were awakened with knocks at our cabin's door. The voice then said: You must have the shot. You can't leave the ship without it.

Out of the cabin, mom and I were met by two men. The man in the brown suit, and the ship's maintenance man. Mom got hers first. She flinched a little. Getting mine felt nothing. I had to give some thought of the boy who seemed so hurt by his shot as Illusions.

Retrospect: The illusionary way could very well be is that when we left the Italian town of Naples or where-ever we were, after the greased pole game and the movie, we then re-entered the "ship", but I don't recall re-entering the "Brown". Then, mom and I went into a deep sleep across the Atlantic Ocean until we reached the Port of New York, the voyage of 5-7 days. It is all speculation on my part, but it makes as much sense of an otherwise absurd story.

My next remembrance was the banging on all the doors, as if there were more passengers besides us. The lone crewman then let it be known: "The trip is over, you are to leave the ship!" It seemed strange that the reliable ships intercom didn't have anything to say first with the message prior to the "crewman's" announcement. Maybe it came on; like other times, but had I slept through it? I may be making more out of what is just part of the *"Script"*. Mom then sat up and asked, "We can leave?" I either said yes or just nodded. We were quickly out of our cabin somewhat followed the same and only crewman. There was no one behind or in front of us. We had to exit the ship's entrance by way of the dining room, I saw only a man's leg entering. As we neared the dining room, I then knew its location. The same lone "ship's crewman" had the final orders for us, "leave the ship through the dining room and there you will get a complimentary drink!" As we entered the dining room, I saw no others except a man's leg then exiting the dining room and presumably the "ship". The same dining room woman "employee" I had once seen before was still behind the counter. Was that man's leg purposely vague, again via divine humor? Of course, I believe it.

As instructed, mom and I stood at the counter waiting to be served our "complimentary drinks." The woman behind the counter told us, "You will have to wait. I have something to do first!". As we waited, I didn't see her doing anything but standing still.

While we waited, I "just happened" to look over my left shoulder and saw my near hero kid again. He was seated and looked toward me. He still wore only trousers, and his short sleeve shirt. He had a sad look about him and maybe I had the same sad look about me. We seemed to be in the "same boat," literally and figuratively. Sitting next to him was a woman of complete contrast. She wore an ear-to-ear smile, a beautiful fur coat and was well made up with lipstick and all, could she had been his mother, I

thought. Why were they the only ones still on the ship? What were they waiting for? The woman didn't even give me a glance. Mom seemed to be oblivious to it all, just waiting for her free drink. Of course, as usual I said nothing to her about my concerns. And of course I thought that my near hero boy and his mother were Illusions.

Our complimentary drinks arrived. They were small Dixie Cups with Pepsi Cola. They held only a few ounces each. Mom seemed as though she would like more. I too would have liked a little more. To drink any more might have meant a toilet issue. (I had never used a toilet for any reason, but that one time, outside up against my bedrooms' wall, It was a false alarm). I very much liked what I drank but it couldn't compare to the magnificent "puddle water" that I slurped at the old castle.

One of the two dining room "employee" made his silent entrance. He seemed to look at no one or anything, just stood there. Mom upon seeing him, being without food since leaving Vasto was probably starving. She rushed to him and in some way or another asked him to get her some food. He quickly returned. He had two plates. We sat at a dining table. It was the first time we ever shared a table or food. The plates each had a small piece of whitish looking something. My thought was swordfish. She immediately made history of her little portion. Then, she eyed my plate that I hadn't touched my piece and with her eyes indicated that she wanted it, if I didn't. I just nodded my head for her to take it. She quickly made history of the few pieces of the food."

Then, unbelievable and without a word, she rushed out of the dining room and was out of sight, leaving me sitting there. Did mom hear someone call for her that I didn't hear? There was no excuse for it, unless she wanted to lose me. I continued to consider myself as persona-non-grata, to all except the power that I didn't know, Other than My Great Paper Airplane Maker. More likely a message from DIVINE POWER.

CHAPTER 20
Port of New York: Sometime 1946

When mom took off on me the way she did I didn't consider my lack of normal senses. It could easily have been that someone outside the ship called out to her and I didn't hear it. Angry at her as I made my way out of the ship.

Below were mom and a woman hugging each other. It would be her sister, with a problem of her own. Next to them was a boy about my age, he would be my cousin. He did have a smile for me. I didn't return his smile. There was nothing there for me. Not even an acknowledgement of my present there.

Then, my near hero kid and the woman in a fur coat came rushing down the gangplank. She pulled on his arm as if in a rush. They would approach a reddish building, never to be seen by me again. Unlike his mother dressed for the cold the boy had a short sleave shirt.

If all were normal, there would be at least someone from U.S. Immigration/Naturalization Service to direct and document us. Absolutely nothing like that happened. I have no idea what mom had in terms of documents for us. Italians were noted to be without papers (w.o.p.).

The two women continued speaking and in Italian, but I couldn't understand a word. Then, my aunt changed to speaking in English.

It was more confusion for me. Did I hear aunty change the conversation from Italian to English or was she still talking in Italian and as usual, it got converted to English for us via mental telepathy or Designed Illusions. It would be consistent with my aunt's arrogance, showing off her English, but not realizing that we could understand her every word, in English.

Aunty and my cousin didn't have a single word for me. Aunty never gave a glance my way. Mom didn't introduce us.

I don't want to give my aunty more credit than she deserves. I understood her as she told mom, while pointing to a man sitting in a parked sedan, "You must rush, my neighbor will drive you to your train, we will talk later! It was nice of aunty to set it up.

Once at the grand central station auntie's neighbor was gracious to take us to the train station and even gave the conductor our tickets.

I don't think Mom could have handled it all herself. In short order, the train left the station. It was as if it waited on us. I believe that mom and I had guidance all the way via DIVINE POWER.

Retrospect: I would be unappreciative not to say something nice about my aunty. After all the work she must have put in to get mom and me to America for mom to be re-united with dad. But I must still think not long and hard to appreciate her. She would want too much in return for her work, not just money. Aunty and I would never get along. She made sure of that. Anyway. I believe it was all Via DIVINE POWER anyway.

CHAPTER 21
Final Leg:
Sometime 1946

I remember very little of the train ride other than the aggravating clack, clack of the old type rails and mom's continuing silence. Maybe in about four hours, we were in Washington, D.C.' Union Station.

I was very impressed with the structure of union station and its tall ceiling. I remember seeing nothing and no one as we walked through Union Station. We soon were approaching the taxi stand. A lone cab and driver is there as if he is the only one to take us. Mom handed him a note probably provided by aunty. The driver quickly read it and nodded his head as if he understood it all. He never said a word, or us to him. I knew nothing of a motor vehicle. It seemed to me the cab continued on without ever stopping for any reason. He knew exactly how to get to our destination.

I saw a sign saying that we were in Prince Georges County, in Maryland. I was instantly taken by a building on my left that had the same architectural structure when we were in Naples or whatever Italian town. It was a movie theater. I had hoped that we wouldn't end up too far from there.

I could tell that we were nearing the end of the ride. The driver continued to look forward then quickly turned left into a narrow street. The driver stops in front of many concrete steps going upward. a woman up on the hill frantically waving to the driver. Our voyage was over. Another bad voyage was about to begin. Up on the hill in front of a house were five people. Three young ladies in a cluster, a short woman and a skinny, short balding man, I assumed it to be Dad. He looked very familiar. He very much looked like that of the lone soldier in dress uniform sitting on steps, never giving me a look as I walked past him. The lone man up the hill wouldn't look our way, but away from us still in the taxi. The man got a nudge from the lone woman to look at us.

As the taxi came to a complete stop, mom rushed out and quickly up the many concrete steps. Immediately she was in the arms of the man. She gave him many hugs and kisses as I again felt like persona-non-grata. Dad returned mom's affections in a nonchalant manner. That had a big effect on me. It said to me that we weren't welcomed in his life. I wanted to be anywhere but there. The thought of New York and maybe to just continuing walking seemed the better alternative.

I waited for some instructions from the hill. Mom leaving her little suitcase in the cab gave me reasons to remain in the taxi until I got some acknowledgement from my father. One of the girls waved at me to exit the cab. Dad wasn't interested in me.

I looked up at Dad. He continued to ignore me. I pressured him for eye contact, but it was only with the woman's encouragement that he looked at me. When he did, he looked at me with a frown. I was crushed. I would never address him as father or dad until he earned it. I never addressed him as father or dad.

One of the girls rushed down to get me out of the taxi. She was irate at me for remaining in the taxi and causing additional fare. I looked at the driver for his input. The driver just shook his head (no). The girl asked the driver for the price of the trip, The driver had not said a word the entire time and just shook his head again (nu) to the fare. I glanced down at the small suitcase that mom had left behind in her haste to reach dad. It somewhat smoothed things over with the girl and others on the hill.

On the hill in addition were two other young ladies. The entire "cast of "characters": Mom, dad, dad's Sister-in-law, LUNA. The 3 cousins: Oldest, Middle and Youngest. The tallest and largest, was my middle cousin. She was an Amazon in comparison to the rest of us. She appeared to be second-in-command.

Uncle, Dad's brother and husband to Luna and the breadwinner, but not the head of the household was still at work when we arrived.

Everybody had congregated to enter the house. Mom and dad went first.

Retrospect: The taxi driver at Union Station, D.C. knew precisely how to get to the house. Not charging a fare. I often thought what if that driver didn't know his way and got lost. I consider the route a complicated route. He knew it perfectly. Mom and I couldn't help the driver should he have needed it. Considering all, was the driver also placed by DIVINE POWER?

CHAPTER 22
From the frying pan: Sometime 1946

Mom had already pushed dad into a bedroom, or his own bedroom, There were giggles among the girls. Luna gave orders that her girls stop giggling. Then Luna gave the orders for all to go into her house.
We all walked single file inside. The girls disappeared into their bedrooms. I sat on the sofa. Still no desire for anything. Then, LUNA let it be known by yelling out of the dinner she had prepared for all of us. We quickly complied and sat at the dining room table. Then I knew who the power in the house was.

Sitting at the table looking at totally white were what may have been Italian cheese on my plate. Luna kept gazing at me angrily. She had to ask: "What's wrong?" I told her that I couldn't eat it. The others at the table ate theirs. She took my piece and ate it. Then, she told me: "You don't eat" She meant while I was at her house. Mom got brave, went to the kitchen and quickly made a couple strands of pasta for me. I ate them. Luna wasn't happy at that. The white pieces of cheese was all there was to eat for all.

Luna gave orders for all to go to their rooms. She looked at me in hatred and pointed to a nearby door.

You go up there. On the way up, the heat quickly overtook me. It got worse as I reached the top. I was in the attic. The ceiling was so low that I had to crawl on my hands and knees to get around, and of course, the attic was also used for storage. At the far corner was a little thin mattress. I crawled over to it and lied down to test it out. It had an odor and felt damp. The mattress was a problem but mostly, the overpowering heat was what wouldn't allow me to sleep. I crawled over to the little triangular shaped window to open it and allow cold air in the attic, but it wasn't made to open.

Victoria then came up the steps and was stopped from going further by the low ceiling. Then she asked, "How do you like it up here?" It was a dumb question overall. She spoke to me in English. Didn't she know that I had just

"Gotten off the boat," but I answered her, "It's too hot up here"! I had just spoken to Luna in verbal English for the first time in America. It was all in fluid English, no more mental telepathy if it ever was? Maybe trying to digest my answer spoken in English, she hesitated, and then said, "That's all I got!" She then proceeded to return downstairs. I must have given thought that I was experiencing being uncomfortable for the first time, other than my aching knee when returning from the farm, I now consider it all as Spiritually Commanded.

It is interesting to again note that as an Italian kid directly from an offbeat Italian town, I conversed only in English and Luna was not at all impressed, as the entire household wouldn't be. If they were impressed, they never showed it nor ever asked me about it. Another sign I was again persona-non-grata. I was just not welcomed there.

It was too hot to stay in the attic. I followed Luna down to the very comfortable first floor. She was surprised at seeing me behind her. She told me "Alright, you can stay down here for now, but you have to go back upstairs!" I didn't answer her and sat down on her very comfortable sofa. She even turned the little glass screen at the corner of the room, as she told me that, "It's called television." She turned it on. I liked my situation then. I was watching a Cowboy Movie. She saw that I was enjoying it then turned it off. I sat on the sofa and lo looked at the walls.

Luna was trying to tell me how evil works, give a little to someone who has nothing then quickly take it back.

Reluctantly, because of the heat there, I only dared to go back into the attic. Once there though happiness set in that the attic was no longer hot but felt good. I went over, as in normal and tested the mattress again. It was also good for laying on it. I again was without normal senses.

I went back down to the first floor. Uncle was there with my father. Both seem to enjoy a drink from uncle's stash of liquor in his liquor cabinet. Uncle asked me if I wanted a drink. At 8 years old I knew nothing of liquor. I shook my head (no). Dad had nothing to say to me, or even give me a look. Uncle fixed himself anther of what he called a "highball" and offered to make one for me. A highball is still an alcoholic mixed drink. I turned him down again, but he insisted. I drank it. I didn't know then that it should have had an effect on me it didn't. Maybe, he didn't include the gin. In Uncles stocked liquor cabinet I could even read some of the bottles: Gin, Black Label (scotch),

Anisette (a liqueur) and Vermouth. Mo beer seen. I didn't know then that I wasn't supposed to be able to read. (How would a kid just out of World War 2, with the schools closed and no remembrance of his first 7 years on earth, able to speak understandable English?) I never gave that a thought. I just spoke when I needed to. I had at least the same knowledge as most kids my age, but without school/training. The "highball" was my first drink since the shot of Pepsi on the "ship."

In Vasto, Italy mom did attempt to enroll me in a class probably that had just reopened at the end of the war. I then heard Mom and the teacher speak in a language that I couldn't understand, (Italian). It freaked me out and I followed Mom out of the building. It didn't matter because we soon left for America. Anyway, I have doubts that Mom had the money for that school.

Victoria gave mom and me a cheap tour of her partially finished basement "We use it for entertaining!" she yelled out. I couldn't imagine her entertaining anyone who wouldn't quickly become sick of her. But the basement felt cool, a contrast to once the attic. I thought that I would be able to use it as a respite. Down deep, I knew that was wishful thinking.

Mom had her faults as well. She never even tried to be gracious to anyone, but I had to stand with mom, the better of the two. It didn't matter much, because Luna was what she was. She stood tall and everybody else was underneath her. Maybe even her 3 daughters.

As I had suspected would happen, Luna called me into the kitchen. I had to do kitchen duty as the girls went about their business. It was pure and simply another of her dominant stance. Then, with a little show of compassion and without me asking her, cousin oldest daughter took over for me and even turned on the television for me. had some angry words for her oldest indicating displeasure with that move. A few minutes later, the T V was turned off and gave me a cold stare as she walked away from the T V.

Mom and I not long ago had come out of World War 2. I never was quizzed of my experiences in the war. Of course, if I was asked, what could I tell them? That I didn't know anything of the war? I experienced only some illusions of war.

I was sitting on the sofa and still not at all sleepy, as everyone went to their respective sleeping quarters. Mom and dear dad were already in theirs. I had lost all contact with mom. She stayed mainly in her room and would try to win dad back.

Victoria came out of her bedroom and ordered me to the attic: "Go upstairs, go to sleep!" I had to comply. Though I had to crawl there all good with temperature for me.

I don't know if I was aware that then I had almost lost my immunity to the elements or if I ever had immunities. I did know that I had never experienced discomfort before. When I entered the stairwell to the attic, I left the door open to rob the first floor of some of its cool temperature. Luna slammed it shut. I really thought that I was going to the attic to die. However, as I reached the attic, I was totally comfortable. I sat at the edge of the floor with my legs dangling in the stairwell. I was again "bewitched, bothered, bewildered" I was very happy that I would survive the attic. I crawled to the mattress and fell fast asleep. The attic would never be a problem for me again, nor any of its temperatures. All happened on the first day at Luna's house.

One day as usual, I was standing outside. Cousin Marcy came rushing out and admonished me for being outside without a coat: "Aren't you cold?" she demanded to know. "No!" I replied. She said, "Well, it's too cold for you to be out without a jacket, I'll get it for you!" She quickly came back with my jacket and at the same time told me, "I can't believe you're outside without a jacket and with only a short sleeve shirt!" Marcy had freaked out by it all, I didn't mean too. I could have thought, finally I was totally comfortable, again without trying.

It seems that my immunity to temperature were restored. I could also ask: Why did it have to be taken away? No other reason, but DIVINE POWER.

CHAPTER 23
Diet By Design: Sometime 1946

One day I felt hungry for the very first time. Food had never entered my thoughts until then. I believe it was a DIVINE set up. I don't know the time frame since Luna's' "welcome dinner." I looked in her refrigerator then put some available luncheon meat between two pieces of bread. Unknown to me then, it is called a sandwich.

Just as I was about to take a bite, Luna upon seeing me, verbally chastised me as she grabbed it out of my hand and continued with her barrage. From that point on, or sooner, I would never be fed again, Luna had already said that to me before. At Luna's house I think it was her plan. Little did she know that I could be good eating, or not eating, I still didn't know the difference until I had hunger pangs, no doubt from the will of the DIVINE. But to be fair, no one in the house had much money as dad, no money.

The question has persisted why, as never before, had I suddenly experienced hunger pangs, normal for sure, but not for me, never up to that point. Luna "conveniently" was there to stop me.

At some point, not eating got the best of Marcy. I was sitting on the couch and could see Luna in her kitchen. Marcy came in the front door and gave me a stare. She looked distressed and came to query me: "Have you eaten anything?" I was surprised by her query and concern. I only shook my head: (no). She rushed over to her mom, then to my mother who almost lived in her room. Mom then rushed out and as she walked, yelled out the incredible revelation and to whoever could hear: "He Never Ate In Italy!" No doubt, me not eating had concerned mom for many years. She then quickly returned to her room. Luna had mom in total room confinement. Mom in some ways caused it on herself.

Luna, it seemed impressed with mom's "earth shattering" utterance, me eight years without food (liquid as well). It didn't seem to be of interest to anyone except my mid cousin. No one would ever query me about that statement. No matter what, no one cared for me the persona-non-grata.

Mid cousin would make an attempt to feed me even upon my objection. She took me to a "sandwich shop" where a male friend of hers worked, and I was treated to a "hoagie" (sub). I had eaten it all.

My mid cousin made a nice, but unwanted food. Not long after that sandwich, it created a new problem for me. I had a need that I never expected or experienced before. I had to use the toilet. I looked around to make sure I was alone. I didn't want Luna to know. I just knew she wouldn't like me using her bathroom.

I wanted to be quick, but I had some difficulty. I overstayed my time in the bathroom. Soon, Luna was banging on the door acting insane. I was quickly out as she continued with her tirade about her bathroom being used. I would never use her toilet again. I think a few times though; I quickly used it standing-up due to drinking water from a hose that I used for watering the lawn. (I can still taste the material of that hose). A few times, I went on the side of the house. Were my natural senses slowly becoming normal? No.

CHAPTER 24
Personals:
Sometime 1947

I gave little thought as to what I wore, none of my personal hygiene. I wasn't at all concerned at not being "preppy". I didn't think of my clothes or shoes to form an opinion of their condition. One reason was that I was always traumatized. The clothes I wore were probably all I had or would have for quite a while, but they seemed to be holding up well.

I knew nothing of bathing. Bathing was not available to me in Vasto. I had no insight about hygienic and I was not enlightened by anyone. The only water I ever saw was the Adriatic Sea and the illusionary "puddle water" at the old castle. In Vasto, I never saw a drop of rain. I don't remember getting a haircut. Maybe mom trimmed it as I laid in the "coma," but nothing when I was awake. Haircuts would not be in my life for years to come. The very first time I saw my reflection was in Luna's bathroom's vanity mirror on that day of the toilet thing.

M7 mid cousin enlightened me about bathing: "Have you ever taken a bath?" she asked. I was again taken aback by another strange query. More trouble coming my way, I thought. I answered, "No." Marcy told me: "Well it's time you took a bath. I'm going to put water in the tub for you!" I then heard water pouring in the bathtub. I could have thought that at least she first got her mother's permission. I was in the tub of shallow water and soon Luna was blasting her daughter for allowing me to use her tub. Mid cousin quickly knocked on the door and frantically told me to, "Get out of the tub you didn't need a bath anyway!" Once out, Luna was there to give me more of her vicious stares, as if to blame me, again.

Not learning her lesson, Mid cousin let me know that she wanted to wash my clothes. I had to wait in the attic while they partially dried. She didn't tell me if my clothes were torn or worn in any way. She didn't say if any needed mending. My guess is that they held up very good. The walking shorts I wore in Vasto were probably left behind, no room in mom's little suitcase. All Via DIVINE POWER

CHAPTER 25
The Foster Boy: Sometime 1947

My first sight of James the foster boy was when he came through the front door smiling. Then he went straight to Victoria and held out his hand to her. She immediately smacked him. He cried, but he stood his ground. She smacked him again. I still don't know why it was ever necessary for her to do that. James was mentally challenged. He only wanted some food. It turned out it was Luna's responsibility to feed him when he visited. Lucky for James, he didn't have to go to Luna's house in a daily basis. Luna told me, although I didn't ask her, "They don't pay me enough to feed him!" The few times I saw her feed him it was only a small piece of bread. If he asked for more, he might be slapped or threatened with such. Sometimes, she would wait for uncle to return home and tell him lies about James and ordered uncle to administer smacks of his own. I often heard the smacks and the crying James.

Someone was capable standing up to Luna and it was her mid daughter. No one else ever intervened on his behalf except mid daughter. No one else dared. I once saw James get his smacks, instead of a piece of bread, and James went off crying. Marcy got a piece of bread for him, but Victoria took it back.

If I asked Luna for food, I could have gotten the same smacks, lucky for me or maybe for Luna as well. I only had to witness and now report.

CHAPTER 26
Between rock & hard place: Sometime 1947

I took a dry run to the movie theater I had seen when mom and I in the taxi passed by from Union Station, D C on our way to Luna's house. The movie posters were very colorful and impressive. I really wanted to see a movie. The showing was, "Song of the South" in Technicolor. I read the entire poster then went in and checked the price. I could read the poster and the prices of the movies and candies.

I returned to the house and went to ask her the silly question, "Can I go and see a movie?" As expected, "Do you have the money for the movie?"

"No" was my reply. "Then, how do you expect to go to a movie?" She said that I would have to wait for uncle to get back from work and hit him up. It had to be uncle; dear dad said he had no money. I know it because one evening as I sat alone in the front room, dad came in from his room. He sat across from me, and as usual refused to make eye contact. I thought it could be my responsibility to "break the ice." The house was preparing to play penny-ante poker. (I was told it was an annual thing). I went over and asked him, "Are you going to play?" He replied by shouting it out, "I ain't got no money!" then quickly returned to his room. He hated me, but I didn't know, why? Once I was told by mid cousin that dad was interested in another woman while in the U.S. military and that I was in the way.

Years in the U.S. military, why he couldn't save money? He then had the girlfriend in his life. She probably got it all. He probably thought that he had gotten rid of mom and me. Considering my "coma's" in Vasto, Italy, he may have thought I would have died. I would learn that he wasn't approachable. Mom would have to be my go-between.

Just as uncle was about to walk up to the front door I asked, "Can I have money for a movie?" Surprisingly he said, "Sure, how much do you need?" I said, "Sixty-five cents." "What's playing?" he asked. "Uncle Remus!" I mistakenly told him. I got the sixty-five cents and fifteen extra. I knew how to count U. S. money; I easily knew that I had the correct amount). The movie was very memorable. I found my exit out of the mad house. Down deep, I knew Luna would step in, hard at some point. Then Luna came to me completely out of it! She told me to never ask her husband for money again.

Sometime passed and another movie was called for. Again, it can only be possible with uncle. I again waited for him to return from work. I asked, "Can I have money for a movie." "Okay" was his reply. I got the exact amount, nothing extra that time.

I waited outside thinking there would be some repercussion for my bold move. unexpected, I also heard from dear dad. He came rushing out snorting fire. From a distance, he verbally tore into me. I felt that if he could have gotten away with it he would have killed me then and there. He was totally on Luna's side.

I waited outside to give people time to cool off. Once inside, Luna of course had to have the last say: "What makes you think you could go behind my back and get money from my husband. Who do you think you are?" I needed to reply, "I'm bored, there is nothing for me to do here!" She had the last word, "That's too bad!" Dad came out of his room to glare at me. Maybe then I needed intervention from THE DIVINE.

A few days passed and more strangeness. Totally unexpected Luna came to me while I was outside and handed me ten silver dollars. She said here, they're from my parents across the street, "Go there and thank them" . I really wasn't that grateful for the generous gift. It made me feel like a charity case, which of course I was. What was I expected to do with them if not use them for movies? I felt there would be repercussions if I spent them. It felt like a trap. Silver dollars then were not viewed as collectibles items as they are now. They were very worn and the same date. I knew all that about silver dollars. They weren't very collectable.

Undaunted, I used the silver dollars for movies in quick succession. Walking back after another movie, mid cousin met me out in the street. She asked, "Where have you been?" I was surprised by the question, but I suspected why she was there. I replied, "To the movies!" She told me, "You can't go again, unless somebody goes with you!" A trick question for sure, someday I would have to call her on it.

Once in the house of course, Luna tore into me about spending the silver dollars. Later, when uncle got back from his work. He had something to say too, "Money burns a hole in your pocket!".

I was kept from going to another movie although I accumulated some unsolicited quarters from first cousin. I asked mid cousin if she wanted to go see a movie with me. As I expected got a quick "NO!" like in the movie, she pulled a "Catch 22."

I never cried before until I was alone with my oldest cousin who supplied quarters in my pocket, but I was not allowed to leave the house of pain for another movie and I just lost it. It was long in coming.

One day while outside, mid cousin came out with a message most likely ordered by Luna, "Your father is going to divorce your mother. He met a woman in Oregon when he was in the Army. He likes to dance with her. Your father loves to dance!" Then she quickly returned inside. It was a payback for going to movies and spending my silver dollars. I was dumb founded and was left to ponder. My thought was that it happened during the war. When the war ended many soldiers returned with better everything compared to dad's stupidity.

It made sense that it was the reason he hated me. If not for me, he could have divorced mom. What didn't understand was why they were spending so much time together? They tried, but didn't work out? Then I thought about the other woman." It would be laughable if it wasn't so very serious. What did the other woman see in dad? He was short, skinny, balding, illiterate, broke, no job and no job skill, not good looking and had a temper. But he did love to dance, a playboy mentality for sure. It may have gotten him over the hump with her. After "Song of the South," none of the other movies measured up anyway.

CHAPTER 27
Blast from the Past: Sometime 1947

I was engaged in my usual and very acceptable activity, sitting and looking at four walls. An attractive young lady of about sixteen came rushing through the front door. She immediately sat and just glared at me. I recognized her. I had seen her a few times before. She was another cousin from dad's side who arrived in America along with her brother about six months after mom and me. I knew her as a cousin only because she once told me so. I was then still only barely eight years old. She spoke only Italian. I didn't speak Italian nor understood her. My cousin couldn't understand me, and I didn't have an answer for her, even if my life depended on it.

She angrily looked at me and had to ask in Italian, "Do you speak Italian?" I might have understood that much and just shook my head (no). I was getting perturbed that I also sensed hostility by her demeanor. She seemed psyched that I didn't remember her from Italy. Thankfully mid cousin came in, sat between us, and answered her queries for me. "He doesn't remember you and only speaks English!" She said to her. Then, mid cousin left, as did my Italian born cousin. She left the house still angry with me. Sad, that the adults didn't properly introduce us. Oh yeah, I was still persona-non-grata.

It would have been nice if someone had taken the time to bring us a little closer together by addressing our differences, but she was an arrogant young lady and I don't think it would have mattered. The next time I saw her was when she got married. Like a bad movie, she again entered the house, flashed a big diamond ring at me, and wore a fur coat. She then spoke a little English. She was there only to flaunt it in my face. I wasn't at all impressed with her. She would be the same next time seeing her and the last time many years in the future. She forever hated me. But in her favor, I heard that she had opened an Italian restaurant and was very successful. It is only speculation. She, along with adults visited me in Vasto. I was then in the "coma" state and was forced to awaken and be introduced to the visitors. More than likely, I did my part at appearing normal to the visitors. The problem was that my eyes were open, but not my brain. I might have been at the age when I should have had remembrance of others. I had no recall until I awoke on my own and my first sight was mom and grandma almost seven years after being born. The *"Script"* probably needed to be followed, completely.

Retrospect: A similar situation years in the future when Mom came to me with a photo of me at about a year of age. It was a picture taken in a studio. I had on a sailor suit probably supplied by the studio. I was sitting, looking straight into the camera. I thought I was cute, so what was the problem? Mom was eager to let me know that she didn't consider me cute, but very bothersome at attempting to have that picture of me on that day. She said, "Oh, you were so much trouble taking this picture, you wouldn't believe!" Unfortunately, I didn't ask her to explain. I was still very angry with her for the beach fiasco. (She never apologized for her part attempting to off me, nor ever brought it up). My guess is being in a "coma" I kicked-up a storm at being taken out of my element. I probably was not to be disturbed for any reason. Mom being a mom had to have it her way. After all, a mom wants a picture of her youngster. Thankfully, then I calmed down long enough to have the picture taken.

Maybe Dad was still in Vasto at the time and also tried to control me. It is only my guess, mostly a good guess.

CHAPTER 28
And Baby Makes Four: Sometime 1947

I was outside when an unusual sight came in view, mom and dad walking up the concrete steps. Mom was carrying a small bundle. It was strange seeing them together. Not since the first day of arrival at the house of pain that I saw them together. Neither one looked at me, the persona-non-grata, as they went into the house. I thought the bundle was food that they decided was needed at the house.

One day I was sitting on the couch facing Victoria's bedroom. Mom then sat on Luna's bed doing something to the bundle that she had brought in the house. I could only imagine Luna seeing mom sitting on her bed and at least making a big thing out of it. It was Luna's way. She didn't want mom, me and dad un her home. I took an end run and snuck a peek into the bedroom. On the bed was a baby girl, mom changing her diapers. I couldn't believe it; I had a sister. Never mind we couldn't afford food or anything else for my HER.

I was still only 8 years old I had no prior knowledge of the "blessed event." I had never seen a pregnant woman before and just as likely, I didn't know where babies came from anyway. I never gave it a thought. After all I claim that any other than grandmother and uncle that I saw in Vasto, Italy were only illusions to me? Of course, I believe, Yes.

I didn't appreciate yet another problem; at least it probably helped keep Dad. I was not happy for the new arrival. I just couldn't understand another person being put in what I considered a potentially devastating situation. What would become of us if anything happened to dad, he was it. There would be absolutely no one to step in of any trustworthiness. Mom could never make a living for us.

One day I was sitting on the sofa next to the door as dad walked in. I saw that he had a small plastic blue and white toy flute. He might have found a job and bought it. He looked at me and I saw his first smile, direct at me, strange sight itself. I thought the flute was for me. Then, cute last cousin came in the room and she got the flute. I was devastated. He had shown a sadistic side. It was just another insult, for which I would never forgive him.

Retrospect: I don't know why I knew it was a flute. I never saw a flute before. I could also visualize crabs clinging to a drowned body and not having seen a crab before, the same with visualizing a swordfish with the long bill and all and never seeing a swordfish. Again, I knew the same or more than anyone else my age did. Although I claim that, I remember nothing for almost the first seven years of my life, all by the grace of DIVINE POWER

CHAPTER 29
More from the P-Nut: Sometime 1947

I was again spending time outside. Uncle and Luna wearing their best returning from somewhere, nor did I care. I made the mistake of looking at her. She angrily yelled at me, "You need to go to church too!" Uncle just looked away seemingly not wanting to get involved. It might have been the first time that I saw them doing the Sunday ritual. My guess is that it was a nice day for a walk and that would lead to the church.

I wanted to say, "hey idiot Luna what is church?" I knew nothing of religion. I was never introduced to religion or a church. Why did I need to go to church? What had I done that is so bad that I needed to go to a church? I bet Luna knew.

It is said that the nearby Saint James Catholic Church and elementary school was somebody's inspiration for the movie, "The Exorcist is about a boy overtaken by demons in the early 1940's when he attended the Saint James parochial school. And, Georgetown, D.C., being only about a half hour away by car. Did Victoria mean that I needed exorcism? No, back then it wasn't known as such to the average person.

CHAPTER 30
Chesapeake Bay Trip: Sometime 1948

Without reason, or purpose I found myself In a Chesapeake Bay town near the waters edge. I stood motionless just looking around. I have absolutely no memory of hpw I got to that point happened. Looking to my right side I could see the backs of two women that I recognized as mom and her New York sister. Just ahead of me was a table with prepared food. In a bowl fried chicken pieces stood out. Standing beside the table were two women, One was Luna, the other I didn't know then. She was Luna's sister from another town,

I didn't know where I was, how I got to that exact point. I don't remember being in a car, the only way there.

Suddenly, out nowhere I experienced something I had not experienced before a very intense smell of the fried chicken. I needed some. I called out to Luna for some. She said no. Then her sister told her to give me some. What I got from Luna was a smallest piece in the bowl. I was quick to eat it and left.

I walked into the nearby building. There was dad and uncle doing some serious talking. No doubt it was about our departure from the house. Luna's wish from the start.

There were machines there that I wanted to play but it took coins.

I returned to the little feast but saw no one except mom's New York sister seemingly trying for some food. I think she failed. I believe that the little feast was intended for persons she liked including her three daughters who hadn't showed.

I had then disappeared out of the little Chesapeake Bay's town. Not known as to where unless it's back to Luna's house. All Via DIVINE POWER

CHAPTER 31
Strangers in the Mix: Sometime 1948

I was again sitting on the couch looking at four walls when there was a knock on the door. Without being allowed in, the couple entered. They seemed to be in their forties. My first thought was that they were brave traveling at night and coming in without being announced. They would surely get a taste of Luna's venom.

Instead, Luna was meek and welcomed the couple in. It was truly unusual seeing Victoria humbled. I had to think, what was she up to? Nobody was going to enter her house without at least an announce or with something in it for her. She put on a "good face" even if it hurt.

Of course, I wasn't introduced to the pair and would never know who they were, but they were in charge. They asked for everyone except me to gather at the dining room table.

The man saw that mom wasn't there and asked for her participation. Cousin Marcy quickly got mom out of her room, and then the meeting began. The man and woman spoke only in Italian. I didn't understand a word. I was surprised that the meeting lasted only a few minutes. The woman had the last word as the man made a move for the door. It signaled the end of the meeting.

Luna stopped the man in his tracks and asked him, "Can you put something in the piggy bank?" The man answered her in the affirmative. Luna told her youngest girl to "Get the piggybank!". Cousin left and soon returned with one so large that she could hardly carry it. The jingling could be heard, and I thought many more of my movies in there.

No doubt, much of dear dad's money was in that piggybank. Young cousin had dad wrapped around her little finger. The stranger contributed with a ready folded bill and slipped it in the slot, indicating to me that he expected it and had probably contributed before.

The man and woman were again leaving. I was sitting near the door when he stopped and handed me a box. He had only one word for me, "Here." The same only word used by: "My great paper airplane maker" I was so taken by the gesture that I couldn't find the word "thanks" in my vocabulary. Anyway, they were quickly out the door. I never saw them again. Now I believe they were from an Italian/American community

The box was nicely color printed and had a picture of an airplane on it. In the box were two large metal pieces that simply clipped together to form the airplane. It was nicely painted with proper decals. (I later learned it to be the then new U.S. Air Force C54 used in the Berlin airlift fame).

Then, I had a smile, rare occasion. I looked up and saw Luna transfixed on me with an accentuated frown. Clearly, she was unhappy that I got a toy. It was my only toy not counting the wad of clay at the farm in Vasto, Italy. I could have easily thought, "Why was Luna so upset at me for getting a toy?" Even so that she hated me.

Retrospect: My best guess it that the couple were from an Italian/American organization and were there to welcome mom and me to America, but I really don't know for certain. The man used the lone word "Here," and it has stayed with me, to ponder that single word in my mind. Do I dare associate the "Great Paper Airplane Maker and the Visitor for using that single word, "here"? Both presented me with an airplane, one paper, and one metal!

CHAPTER 32
Miscellaneous: Sometime 1948

Luna thought she could say anything she wanted to me at any time, sexual jokes and songs with sexual innuendoes. She was the only one that enjoyed it. There seemed to be sexual frustrations with all three girls as well. One day mid cous took me to the nearby Saint James Catholic Church and Elementary School to try to enroll me. There, I noticed a little girl following me with her eyes. I didn't think too much of it. Thankfully, it turned out that I was too old and too late for its last grade. A few days later mid cous came to tell me that the little girl was anxious to see me. I just shook my head (no). Sometime later, mid cous came over with the same anxious request; again, I had another no for her and the little girl. Luna of course got wind of it and gave mid cousin a cease and desist order. It was the only time that I welcomed her interference. Mid cous said of the little girl: "She isn't going to like it." Later, mid cous had to admit, "I'm sorry, I should have realized that you are both too young." Luna probably knew that I wouldn't be in her house much longer anyway. Luna would call me "Pat," a nickname for my given name (Pasquale). Everybody followed suit except mom. She had issues with it.

I didn't care, but Mom had deep objection with that: "I named you after my father!" she told me. The name "Pat" would stick with me forever.

Mom never had much to say in Luna's house, but when she did say it. it was always in English. Like me, she shouldn't have spoken English at all. Unlike me, she was bi-lingual. Incredibly, we never brought it up with each other.

My place in Italy didn't have a mirror. I never saw my own reflection until I went into Luna's 's bathroom and used her vanity mirror. I can only surmise that it was then that I saw my own reflections, only because it all became available for me. Otherwise, I never gave my looks a single thought.

There seemed to be sexual frustration among the girls. There were announced "kissing cousins" parties. I was invited to them, but I refused to attend even though we were under the same roof. Being totally traumatized, 8 years old, playing spin the bottle was the last thing on my mind. Related boys that lived far away at the house on the Chesapeake Bay's tributary inlet were invited to attend, but only a few came. My refusal to participate wasn't readily accepted, but I didn't care. The television for me had been turned off long ago for good. I thought no television, no spin the bottle. There were no more parties given.

CHAPTER 33
Leaving Evil: Sometime 1948

Again, I was sitting on the couch minding my own business when the foster boy came rushing in through the front door for his visit and went straight into Luna's bedroom. He then came out with one of her large towels. He used it as a cape probably seeing done on television, somewhere. He then "flew" out of the door.to outside.

Luna was in her kitchen. She didn't see him, but I could see and feel many slaps coming to the special ed kid.

James also had a problem remembering the many slaps that he had to suffer through, Or he was truly a "brave" kid. I would always worry about him.

I looked through a window and was able to see him climbing up the elevated laundry drying platform with clothes drying lines. I knew that he was going to climb up and "fly like superman." He would be hurt by it.

I had to go out and stop him. Once I went out to special ed boy, I knew I would also be in more trouble with Luna, She would also blame me. I could have turned the kid in to Luna and maybe had gotten some points for myself. It was much too late in life for that.

Once out, I confronted the boy and told him to return the towel. He paid me no mind. He was about to climb up to the concrete platform. Luna of course got wind of it and came out to claim her towel. She ordered James inside, smacking him for his terrible deed as he walked away.

She had the choice words for me: "You're the problem here!"

When uncle returned from work that day, Luna corralled him in the dining room. I heard her tell uncle half-truth and total lies about me. I thought that I knew of her meanness, until I heard talk to uncle. Then, I knew more of how evil works. When all else fails, lie.

What about uncle? He had been with Luna for many years. Didn't he know how much she lies? How can anyone be trusted when lying is second nature? Did he sell his soul for her? He was robbed. At that point, if not in the future, again persona-non-grata with uncle as well.

I can't blame Luna for wanting her life back. Mom and I were dad's responsibility. He was probably doing the best he could with what little he had going for him. However, lucky for mom and me, he was a proud man. Maybe a lesser man would have just given up, packed-up and left. Maybe, his hatred of me is that he felt the need to stick around for me., being a proud man, he may have had something to prove to himself as well. What bothers me most is that I was so easy for him to ignore. Mom with dad had to permanently stay in their bedroom. He had nowhere else to go anyway.

Mom and I spent a little over two years with Luna and her family. I never kept a diary, but it was what Luna had said to me annually, 2 times, "Its cleaning time!" Moving a few pieces of furniture around and dusting, just a little would do. It would equate to 2 years at Victoria's.

My next remembrance was standing in the front room dressed the same as when I left Italy. It was traveling time, again. Mid cousin came and told me to wait outside.

Mom, Dad and the baby came out too. They proceed down the concrete steps not once looked at me. Then, mid cous came out with the message for me: "You're going to your own house in Washington, you've been enrolled in a school that's close to the house, you're better off there!" Mom and I would be, but dear dad?

Of course, Luna came to me with the last word. "You've got to be a help to your father" Nice of her to put pressure on me, a 8 years old. I would be with the man who hated me. I intended to do little as possible help to him until he changed toward me. My strategy for survival was to stay away from him as much as possible. He should appreciate me keeping my distance, He, being a proud man.

The special ed boy somehow got known of my leaving, came out of somewhere, passed us, sobbing. He ran into the house sobbing. I would not see him again. I looked toward Luna standing by. She had a smile. I agreed with that smile.

I could only hope that mid cousin would see to spec ed boy's well-being." And maybe with me being out of the house he would get better treatment, and being the only boy left. Maybe DIVINE POWER will see to him for me. I would never forgive the rest of the house for not standing up for the special ed boy. II looked up at mid cousin as if a plead to her. Surprising, she told me: "I will look after him"

I entered the sedan that waited for me. It was driven by First cousin. Again, there was not a look my way as I entered the car. It again indicated that I was still persona-non-grata.

Within half an hour, we were at our house in Washington D.C. It was an old Victorian style townhouse. Across the street was the Saint Aloysius Catholic Church and Parochial School (soon defunct). I would attend the end of the $7^{th\ year}$ and the entire 8th and last grade, Then, the school closed for good.

I wouldn't be accepted for enrollment at the school if I couldn't at least speak and understand the English language. I could also read well enough without any training.

But, there too, I was a persona non-grata due to unpaid tuition.

Recapping my food intake while in the 2 years at Luna's house. Started off with 2 strings of pasta, small hoagie (Sub), about 8 figs (off a tree), About 7 steamed snails, a little chicken drumstick at a Chesapeake Bay town. I never had food craving.

CHAPTER 34
Stranger than fiction:

One day in my early thirties I was taken from somewhere, then placed somewhere else to watch a pair of legs easily dropping from a clear blue sky. In no time I could see the entire body of the man as it continued downward. In no time it landed straight up. His back to me and not making a move or sound. I had no choice but to go to him, When I got close to him I turned into him completely. I don't know why it happened that way. All Via DIVINE POWER

I could see a building just ahead of me. I was getting scared and angry at the same time being there. I turned to look to my right seeing only line of small stores, one with the name of a bar. To my left, again just small stores. I was alone, nothing else around me. I didn't know where I was. I had some interest in the bar, but then its name was blurred. I would go in the bar and have a beer and ask for directions. I didn't check for the money to pay for it. I had been taken over, again anyway.

Entering the bar I quickly saw an empty seat at the bar. The bartender came over I told him I wanted a beer. He brought back a beer an glass. He didn't ask me what kind of beer or for payment.

Looking at me was a woman in her late forties sitting with a drink, an empty seat and a young man to her right. No conversation between them. Next time I looked at her she was giving me a stare that said she was interested in me. Me not of her. She left her seat and went around the bar, stopped briefly to chat with the bartender. Maybe even pay for my beer. She continued on her way out but stopped to talk to me. She told me that she wanted me to go back home with her. She told me that she was the manager of the apartment building across the way. I didn't want to go with her, but I needed to know where I was. Asking the bartender never entered my thought. Having sex was the reason at being invited to her apartment.

It was a quick walk for her, For me no knowledge of the walk as we stood at her front door, She was putting her key to the front door as I looked at about the ten concrete steps that ked to that point. I was shocked at not using those steps.

Wu were inside her apartment. She quickly went into the bedroom. I could see her undressing, She's on her bed and called me to join her. I took off my beautiful wristwatch and put it on a light table. I quickly undressed and joined her. I quickly finished and told her so. She then yelled out for me to: "get out, get out, leave". I couldn't leave fast enough, Dressed and out of her apartment. At the door and about to close it behind me when I disappeared from there. I never got to ask her as to where I was in her town. It didn't matter, I was out of there, permanently. Again would not use those ten steps.

I was back to normalcy, whatever that means for me, probably nothing.

For a long time I gave thought of that time. I couldn't figure out why the DIVINE would want me do something that resembled normal. I mean having sex is so normal. I was chosen to have sex with her.

Then finally, it came to me a reason? The woman, name unknown, desperately wanted a baby. Her age a factor on that day. She probably didn't know that the DIVINE was in charge of it all. It would also make me a first time Dad. I forgot my watch, but a gift for our newborn,

DESIGNED ILLUSIONS

POST-CHAPTERS

(Post-1)
Sometime 1946.

I was a very bored boy of 8 years old. Television was new to almost everyone then, but to me it was totally new. The owner of the television, without asking her turned it on for me. After only a few minutes of watching a western movie she abruptly turned if off. She always had a sadistic way toward me. She didn't want me in her house. I didn't want to be there either. She was Luna, my father's brother's wife.

(Post-2)
About 1950:

I was still a very bored boy of 12 years old and no longer in the house of evil. Then my family moved from Prince Georges County, MD to Washington D C.

There was nothing to occupy my time, even my parents who had nothing to say to me. I did a lot of trekking to downtown D C, mostly window shop. That too began to bore me.

Walking along the sidewalk to downtown, passing common weather-beaten red brick semi-detached old townhouses. One was of the house my family and I occupied. The only exception was one that had a new silvery façade. I could see the front entrance also renovated. I would always gaze at it as I walked on to downtown for my window-shopping. As I gazed at the renovated building, Just then, a young man had rushed out looking only at me and yelled with a message just for me "You can go in there and watch television, I've been watching it, it's alright, go in there!!". My immediate thought was of who, is that guy and, how does he know I want to watch television? I didn't believe him, but watching television was at stake. He continued running full speed toward me but didn't stop and continued to cross

I street giving no thought to traffic and quickly disappeared from my sight. I wouldn't see the young guy again.

I stopped to gaze at the refurbished townhouse. I needed to determine if I should go in and make a fool of myself for the possibility of watching a favorite western movie. Reluctantly, I walked up to the entrance. On the brick wall was a plaque stating: "Dental Office for Negroes". The front was wide open. I didn't see a door, and slowly walked in. Somewhat ahead of me was the counter and a woman there busily working. Soon, I expected to be seen, and being asked a lot of questions of my presence there That would have to wait as I continued forward.

Then, I stood in front of the counter, but she just continued working not giving me even a glance. Could I not be seen? Or, I just needed to wait a little longer. She frantically went back and forth doing this and that, never a pause. It gave a chance to search for the television. It quickly came into view. Straight ahead was the beautiful console television set. I slowly went to it. I off and on looked at the woman who still busily back and forth in her work. I turned the TV on, then sat on the floor. Immediately a western movie came on/ I was bored no more. I left when the movie ended. I didn't want to overstay my time. But, wanted to return the next day for more western T V. . There were no sounds for me anywhere, including out of the television movie.

I returned the next day. Again, without any disturbance as I continued on to the television set. The same woman there hadn't slowed down her feverish pace behind the counter and still hadn't given me even the slightest look. I made myself at home with another western movies.

Then, I see company. A tall black man entered and made his way past the woman behind the counter to the back where another black man dressed in white garb awaited him. Then, both walked permanently out of (my) sight. I spent a long time watching western movies, until it changed over to other viewing, then I left the "Dental Office" and the woman still behind the counter with her frantic "work" ethics.

On my return home mom gave me a lot of grief as never before of my being away for such a long time. How long was I really gone?

I fully expected to return there for more television, but dad brought home our own television set. It was a very small screen in comparison. Dad was broke. Where did he find the money for my television.

I would never pass by the Dental Office again" Was it all a set-up Via DIVINE.

(Post-3)
Sometime 1951:

At about 13 years old, I stood at the very corner of North Capital and I Street NW, Washington, D C. I had absolutely no clue what I was doing there, or where I had been prior. There didn't seem to be any noise or activity of any kind of my surrounding. I continued to search my thoughts of where I had been prior to being there. But still nothing came of it. It was all very scary.

Then, my thoughts were to the Catholic elementary school just across the street where I had spent an entire year and the school's final year of existence as a school. It was there that I had physical assaults upon me perpetrated by the school's home teacher nun. She recruited whomever students she could. to do the deed. I held my own until she was able to recruit a few from the nearby Catholic high school. The nun never told me as to the why, but my guess she wanted my tuition to be paid. She could have just expelled me. It is also her frustration of her school closing and her sadistic inner self.

Back on the corner, as my mind reverted to the present. I could see my house from across the street. but I didn't see my inoperable bicycle that I had placed on the front lawn, it was gone. As I was about to take the first step toward home, The "Spiritual Being" He told me that I couldn't go there anymore. I thought he had just told me that he was throwing me out of the house. I said to him that I wanted to get some things from my room. He repeated that I couldn't go there (home) anymore but continued that he had found another place where we could stay. It became clear, I feared we been evicted from the house. Probably, for not paying rent.

Where was I when the move out had taken place? I had no clue, but we caught buses toward our new place. We ended at Florida Ave. near a movie theater. I was told for me to walk on the nearby street until I got to the house. He said he would not go with me. The man didn't resemble my dad at all. I proceeded to an extremely long walk. I didn't know how I would find the "new" house without more instructions. Suddenly I ended my walk at a massive amount of train rails. It would be the trains entrance to D C's Union Train Station. But saw no train. I just stood there in desperation until just next to me was a partial opened door. I entered and there was mom, and somewhere newborn the sister. The place was totally without furniture. Then, father emerged from the back door. I couldn't believe he had a smile for me He had managed to save our 12 inch television, otherwise I would be more upset at losing it.. Dad plugged it in for me and I proceeded to watch a western movie. I sense that the house my family occupied was because it was only empty, and that my father knew about it because he had worked on it. The family would move to another house, but not me.

It all will get another DIVINE intervention on my behalf.

(Post-4)

The last thing that I knew, I was very young watching a cowboy movie on our 12 inch portable television set, in that temporary house.

Then, at about 19 years old I stood somewhere on a corner alone looking around to get some knowledge of the area. Nothing came to mind, including a nearby bus stop. I didn't get off a bus. I was dressed nicely to be somewhere that I didn't know where? I was concerned at my position. I was scared. I knew nothing of my next move. All I could do was walk up the street that I stood on. I began my walk. I kept thinking of "4811" as I walked on. I would check the houses for the "4811" house. I came to the end of the street, equal to about 3 blocks from the start.

I could go either left or right on 7th street. I chose the right side, Only, two houses from the corner it revealed the "4811" house.

At the door, after a little knocking I just walked in. The first person I saw was a teenage boy, a few years apart from me. He seemed shocked at seeing me, I couldn't blame him, I was somewhat shocked myself. I knew I was in the right house when I would then see my mother and father. At some point I would see my first-born sister. I only remember her birth. Now as a young teenager. There was also another member I didn't know about another teenage girl, a sister. I was on my parents crap list for not being my fathers helper in his tile setting work. My totally painful knee had me reject that work. To get away from that family life I joined the U S Air Force.

I can only say it was all Via DIVINE POWER,

(Post-5)
About 1960:

About 10 years have passed since I last visited Chesapeake Bay. Then, at Luna's picnic, and all. I had an old clunker, just so I could quench my desire and finally visited the Chesapeake Bay on my own to check out the fishing there.

After traveling on much concrete and asphalt, I was approaching the town of Chesapeake Beach, Maryland. The road suddenly dipped sharply and when it came over the crest, the Bay instantly and as if majestically appeared. Driving with the windows down, another first, the pungent salty sea air quickly filled my nostrils.

It was what I hadn't ever experienced. Not the Adriatic Sea, Atlantic Ocean or with Luna's picnic. Leaving the car and walking at the water's edge, I could also hear the waves crashing on the beach. Then, all my senses were "normal." but would never forget my past. It is constantly on my mind and could bring tears, if I allow it. I don't dare forget.my time being without normal senses.

Another first: I could then see many boats docked and ships navigating the bay. It was more of what I had never experienced before on all other bodies of water. I truly treasured the instant appearance of the bay when coming over that crest of the road. Until, one day the same thing occurred except there was no bay visible. Additional building construction blocked that view/ Almost sacrilegious to me. I thought blocking my favorite sight and visiting the bay again would never be the same.

I was put into normal senses Via DIVINE POWER?

(Post-6)
About 1961:

Then, I was about 20 years old. I was fed up with my unwelcomed, unappreciated job. I drove a long distance to get there. U didn't know It would be the last day at that job.

Walking to my car in the parking lot, nothing indicated inclement weather ahead of me. Everywhere was sunny and warm.

Soon, driving on the main road my car slid everywhere on the road, uncontrollably until I was on the far side of the road. I was stunned at being in that predicament. After all, only a few minutes before I experienced only a nice day. I could see all other cars going by me normally. I was angry, scared and frustrated, at same time. I didn't know what to do to get myself out of it.

Just then, a tow truck pulled up in front of my car. The driver got out, pulled on his winch and walked toward the front of my car. He never looked at me, not even a glance my way. He attached the winch to my car, got back in his truck and proceeded to pull me back on the road.

He then released the winch from my car and rolled it back into his truck. He returned to his truck and simply drove off. Never a word spoken by either of us. No payment required either.

A worthy note, while the tow truck driver did his thing, I saw no other vehicles driving by us on seemingly or stopped for us. I then left the scene, happily on a dry road.

All Via DIVINE POWER?

(Post-7)
About 1969.
Placed in place.

Placed in a strange town: Somewhere, nothing prior of remembrance that I found myself looking up on a perfect sky as two male pants legs were slowly dropping down from the sky. There was no one or anything anywhere. Then, the two pants legs had turned into a full body of a man as it continued on downward. It quickly, easily landed on its feet.

That person just stood there facing away from me. I decided to go to him. When I got to him maybe give some help to "him". That person was me. I stood there very scared of it all, In front of me was a large brick building. Still no people, vehicles to be seen. And all quiet. Not moving, I looked to my right I could only see the row of small businesses buildings.

Seemingly last building had the name of a bar.

I wasn't interested in the bar. Then, looked to my left to see more of the small stores. Looking right again, I saw the same thing except the bar's name was being blurred. I had no clue as to where I was. I decided to go in the bar, have a beer and ask about their town. Never checked for money for the beer.

My short walk there is without memory. Once inside an empty seat was close to the door, The bartender came over to me and I ordered a beer. Asking him for directions never entered my thoughts. Poured some beer in the glass and took a sip. Just across from me was a woman an empty seat beside her then an handsome young man. The woman in about mid forties, or so, She kept looking at me as if interested. I wasn't. She then left her seat walked around the oval bar, stopped to talk to the bartender, probably paid him for my beer. She then continued her walk toward the door then stopped near me. She told me she was the manager at the apartments across the way and that she wanted me to go back home with her, My first thought was no, but I agreed, mostly to find out where I am in the strange town where I had suddenly found myself. I remember stepping outside the bar with her. Then only being with her as she's putting her key in the door's lock. Again, shocked not knowing of the walk there and the not using the many nearby concrete steps leading up to her apartment door.

We are inside. She rushes to her bedroom as I see her disrobing. She put herself in a bed, then calls our for me to join her, Taking my clothes off to join her. We did what we were there for. Normality came, then told her that it was over. She angrily told me to: "Get out, get out, leave. I couldn't do it fast enough. Quickly in my clothes, I would forget my beautiful non-working golden watch. I was quickly outside trying to close the apartment door behind me. I never asked her of where I was. I still didn't have to use those concrete steps.

To ask about my being in the strange place to anyone never entered my thought.

After continued thoughts about being placed in that town I hadn't figured it out, I couldn't imagine The DIVINE imposing such normality without a reason. One day it came to me as the only reason. The objective was for the woman to become pregnant because she desperately wanted a child. As for me, I would be without children knowing I didn't need a child nor wanted one since it would interfere with my knowledge.

Was it all a set-up for me to leave my non-operative golden watch behind in her apartment. A gift to our newborn.
All Via DIVINE POWER

(Post-8)
About 1984:

My job then as a Reproduction Cameraman. I photo reproduced documents at customers requirement. A new day began without any work. I then noticed a bundle not where work assignment would be. A bundle was at a table not used for new work. I couldn't imagine it being there without any personal instruction. That potential work for me seemed to be too thick for reproduction and it didn't have the required work order Thinking that it awaited the work order I would unfold +the document to see a possibility of a job for me. I unfolded it over, over and over until it covered the entire large tabletop. It was a map of Europe. Then, the colorful boot of Italy was right of me with large script words in front of me. I searched for my birth town in Italy. Almost instantly Vasto appeared, and on the Adriatic Sea. It was long ago that my mother had to tell me of my place of birth. Then, I got to know of the where on the map. Vasto, Italy on the Adriatic Sea.

    I refolded the map and put it where I got it. I would not be able to reproduce it, no way should the work order with instructions come.

    The very next day, the first thing I did was look for the map, but it was no longer there. I thought it had been taken back by the person who had placed it there. If nothing else, I got to know more of my town of Vasto. Was the map placed there for my purpose?

(Post-9)
Giving credit to the THE DIVINE

Arriving in America on early 1946 ship that I and mom had boarded named "BROWN" I. couldn't be wrong of its name since I stood on the dock somewhere in Italy and stared right up its huge angled silvery bow. Was it the first time "blurring" was used to make an image purposely unrecognizable. Because I couldn't get the ship's full name, the web search I made was impossible for the reveal of it's full name. But it did reveal of one name ship- still in service as a tourist attraction docked permanently in Baltimore, MD. It is the SS John W. Brown. It is one of twenty-seven hundred liberty merchant ships built by America to carry men and materials to all theaters of World War 2. Incredibly, the "BROWN" is the only ship of its kind that is still afloat and is a Nationally Registered Museum of Historic Places. It accepts visitors and occasionally goes on tour. Photos of the "BROWN" revealed the same ship's huge sharply angled silvery bow and the same large bold lettering at the top/front that I remember very well as the John W Brown.

I was ecstatic at being able to board the ship that brought mom and me to America. Mostly, I could reminisce in my old cabin and the dining room. I had never forgotten about all the illusions in Vasto, aboard ship, and in America. After some failed attempts, because of winter, I finally boarded the "BROWN." Right away, it didn't look right. First, I had to use what is called a gangway to enter. The gangway as seen in war films is flush at the side of the ship. I made it up to the deck, then entered the area where the crewmen huddled around a heater. I told them my reason for being there, that it was the ship that brought mom and me to America. Then, a senior of the group came over and told me that: "Liberty ships didn't carry civilian passengers." I tried to persuade both of us that since the "BROWN" was then making its last trip across the Atlantic Ocean that it got special orders to pick-up stranded American civilians and military dependents along the way. The old seafarer had to concede that possibility. He gave the orders to a crewman and allowed me to venture and "reminisce." Immediately for me nothing at all jelled. The cabin area and the dining room did not exist as I had remembered. I left the "BROWN" and again was totally "bewitched, bothered and bewildered." I must say that I was very upset that only the silvery angled bow and the name "BROWN" is correct.

After some thought that incredibly was the "BROWN" just another illusion? Before leaving the Baltimore harbor, I again stood to view the same bow of the SS John W. Brown, but a totally different ship that I remember well, sometime in 1946.

My next step was to go to the internet again and the www.ancestory.com site to see what else I could find out? A search revealed that a woman and a boy having the exact same names as mom and I arrived at the Port of New York in the same year of 1946, but not the winter month that I recall so vividly, instead it was July, 1946.

The ship that's listed was not the Brown" but one called SS"THOMAS S. BARRY." The search provided not a very detailed photo of the "Thomas S. Barry," but enough to reveal that the ship didn't have the bow, deck or stern configuration that I remember so well.

The big difference is that the "Barry" was a wooden ship as to the Brown metal. "There it is, two ships together didn't equal the ship that I remember.

The "Barry" had no longer existed. "THE BROWN" was a totally Via DIVINE POWER

(Post-10)
About 2004:

My "association" with the DIVINE led me to believe that even without a simple prayer I could look up and say whatever I wanted to the DIVINE, even in anger. The DIVINE is the reason that I didn't get to know World War 2 very much. As in a coma like state until my 7 year. I almost didn't survive then, not the war, but my uncle.

I was near retirement and needed more retirement money that would not be available to me, normal. I thought the DIVINE could have but didn't provide money for me. It made me very angry of the DIVINE that I knew so well. I went to a corner of my room, looked up at where I thought I would be heard. I let it go with sheer anger at the DIVINE. I let it be known that I was through. I returned to watching television.

It began as I drove home the next day. I had bitten one of my fingers, hard. I couldn't believe what I had just done but thought it as a quirk. It wasn't, it was a constant attack on my own finger. A bite had led to another, then to another: Until hearing the knuckle crack of my right index finger. That finger would no longer bend. Then, plucking a piece of bone out of the top of the finger. Very painful as it became as it became infected due to cleaning my aquarium without gloves. My finger couldn't be saved and had to be amputated.

The DIVINE has no pity for insubordinations. "Licking my wound" without anger at the DIVINE.

Was it the DIVINE answering my request in an angry way for help with my retirement finances??.

(Post-11)
About 2005
Just another miracle?

Problems with technical work, there is always new technologies for replacements, thus unemployment was there for me. It seems that there is always an opening for school bus drivers and aides. I would become one.
On one of my special ed routes was a 10 year old girl. I will name Anna. I first got to know her when a boy student was bear hugging other students, then anna. I had to step in and release him from anna. I said good morning and asked Anna if she was ok? But got no response. I sensed a problem. She just didn't seem as though a special ed.

When my bus stopped at the school all aboard went inside, including Anna. Then, the teacher came over to me with her secret. It was about Anna, and that the teacher, I suspect others, had to wipe Anna after her toilet break. I was stunned and couldn't understand the Why? of it. I would try to get closer to Anna and maybe change her ways. Anna's way also was that she wouldn't do any basic things for herself.

Next day, on the bus I went over to Anna with a short song for her. I got a smile and told her my name. You call me call me that., I told her.

She wouldn't have it. She remained quiet. I didn't care I just wanted her to change her ways of doing basic things for herself.

At retirement, no more school bus driving but I still visited her at the special ed school. On one occasion she was at the basement where all other children were celebrating Anna's birthday. Anna wouldn't have any of it. She was alone and stood looking upward. She saw me and came over. I got a cup of ice cream for both of us and two spoons. I gave her a spoon. She said "some" meaning she wanted me to feed her the ice scream. I tried to explain to her she needed to do it herself. She wouldn't have it then slammed the cup to the floor. I left.

On another visit to the same basement location I noticed a teacher nearby sitting with a roll-about desk. I knew the teacher was there for anna. But no Anna. She again stood in a room looking upward. Somehow, we connected, and she came over to me and we sat down. I had to explain to her the advantage of learning and the money factor of learning, I told Anna of what she already knew of the teacher waiting for her. After I thought I said enough

I and she got up. I walked to the exit where the teacher, still there waiting for Anna. I couldn't believe it, I was there without anna, she went the opposite away from me and the waiting teacher.

I had enough, I worry for her, but I wasn't doing her any good, as anyone else in Anna's life. But I had to try once more. I found her standing straight up against the wall looking upward. I gave her a hug and a kiss on the cheek before quickly leaving her for good.

Suddenly, Anne's torso for a few seconds was engulfed with fluttering colorful lights. Then she acted as though coming out of a long coma. She didn't know where she was. She seemed panicky looking everywhere, before realizing that she needed to be with the teacher and the roll-about desk waiting just for her. Anna suddenly realized it and ran there as fast as her legs would take her, Anna quickly sat down at the desk for her. I saw her with a writing instrument in hand. I left her with complete confidence of her change-over.

On that day she became a normal person, or more.

Checking on her in a later time a teacher told me she's "very smart". Nothing to do for Anne after her toilet break.

I decided to check on Anne just to see if she had changed. Once at her school it was the end ot the day, Students exiting including Anne. Sge was heading to a waiting vehicle to take her home. She then saw me and quickly ran to me. Nearing me she spread her arms as if wanting another hug and kiss. I didn't move that way, She decided to give me a hug herself and hung on to my back. She stayed comfortable with that until her waiting horn sounded. She let go of me and quickly went to her waiting vehicle. I would not see Anne again.

Anne was a very needy girl as her mother. I believe her transformation was all Via DIVINE POWER.

(Post-12)
Never a Simplistic Life.

Leaving the pizzeria after my usual slice with anchovies and a glass of beer. A location on a strip mall and a lot of foot traffic There also is movie theater. I was on my way home only a short walk away. Ahead of me were a girl of about 10 years old and an old man. They seemed to be a grandfather and his granddaughter, both neatly dressed.

I just assumed they were at odds with each other. The girl faced one way, the man the opposite way. Both seemed steadfast to their needs. I assumed they were to be somewhere but somehow got themselves sidetracked of their objective. The girl wanted to continue with the search, while the old man dressed in dark suit had given up and wanted to head for home. I knew the area well and thought I could be of some help to them. I walked over and stood between them.

Neither one made the slightest move of my presence. I waited for one of them to respect my presence, but nothing happened. I made a move toward the man to ask if I could be of help. Just then, the girl came to life. She pointed her fingers at the man and insisted that he ask me for the directions. The man turned his head to me and asked: "Do you know where the movie theater is?" I told him that they were just about there and gave him simple the pointed direction to the theater. The man thanked me but, then the girl upon hearing my instructions to the movie theater bolted only to be stopped by her grandfather. He wanted her to also thank me and she did, then bolted again toward the nearby theater.

Grandfather apparently still worn out from their search slowly followed his granddaughter. As it turned out, I found out later the theater offers movies and birthday with parties. Maybe the two had plans for the party and maybe the girl's birthday? It explained her eagerness to be there.

The entire time with the two not a single vehicle or foot traffic came by in otherwise a busy Town Center. DIVINE involvement?

(Post-13)
About 2017:

As an occasional wood worker hobbyist, I had a need for another visit to the local Home Depot store.

Nearing my objective, the red light stopped my progress. At the light, on the medium strip stood an old woman panhandling. Occasionally I give them some money. .And, from her I got the usual: "God bless you!" ".

Then, the light turned green. I was on my way again. Soon, I entered the Home Depot's long, curved driveway. A sunny day then suddenly turned into pitch black, as in a tunnel. I couldn't see anything, and I didn't have the will to apply the brakes. Feeling panicky I opened my mouth to scream but then calmness overtook me. I was good with what was happening. I then leaned back and accepted whatever the DIVINE had in store for me, including death.

I was totally calm and stayed that way for the entire time of about a minute until sunlight again re-appeared and I took over control of my car again. I was nearing a stop sign where I stayed to ponder what had happened and what to do next. I know that driveway has two vicious speed bumps, even the slowest but never felt them. I pondered do I dare make another attempt for Home Depot or not. I went back around and started over to the store. My thought was the DIVINE had fun and it was all normal again. For me, nothing had ever been normal.

I continued for another attempt to the Home Depot. The same panhandler was there at the light which was red again. She asked me if I got lost. I lied and told her I had missed a turn. I proceeded to the store without another "Incident". Now it is about the reason of it All Via THE DIVINE?

(Post-14)
About 2017:

The Home Depot store again, only then I was inside the store. I'm paying attention only of my purchases. I had two items, thinking of another when suddenly I heard my name "Pat" called out. I turned around to see who it was. Two neatly dressed young men stopped next to me. I asked the first one "Do you know me?" He said No. I then asked him "Did you call out my name?" He again said No. Then I looked at the second young man, he also said: "No, not me" I thought, I know.
The two well-dressed young men were store employee salesmen. Nothing to do with bothering me.
END. (Until another visit Via THE DIVINE.

(Post-15)
Mom too, but just aware.

One day I got a call from dad. I didn't give him my phone number because of the same gruff, yelling ways toward me, but only by phone.

He called to tell me that mom wanted to see me. It sensed it to be desperate. We hadn't seen each other in quite a while. A visit was due.

Dad was seated as I walked in. He only pointed to mom, standing. She had a smile for as I walked over to her.

Mom had a message that I totally didn't expect. I knew that like me we experienced conversing in English. We came to America in 1946, from an Adriatic Sea town, Vasto, Italy. There, we conversed only in English. I never knew any other language. Back then Italy and America were at war with each other. Mom just once proved to me that she also spoke Italian, speaking English with me was per DIVINE POWER, otherwise I would be totally lost. Mom quickly and eagerly began with, that nightly her long deceased parents stood at the side of her bed urging her to, "come with us". "Just like you, standing there meaning same as me as a physical sight. According to mom it was a nightly thing. She then said: "How can I go with them?" meaning her still physical being.

Upon leaving, she gave me her only hug. She asked me "Are you going to be alright?" She seemed a little disappointed at my, yes.

She died not long after my visit. of course, I believe what she had to say.

(Post-16)
Sometime 2015
Pull once for happiness.

I returned to my apartment after driving back from a Maryland Casino. I liked playing slot machines. I always began by playing lower amount slots, then move on to the higher amount machines.

But on that day I was physically led to the highest payment machines. There were six seats available with six machines. No one occupied any of the machines I was alone standing at the closest machine to me. I put some money in as my first attempt. I won thousands, next to the biggest amount. The question is how I remember getting to the point of the Casino but only by my nice running car.

Sometime in a 1960's setting I found myself dressed nicely to go out somewhere. I stood in the front room of long ago house in Northeast Washington D C. There was no one else around of the then six people. There was no one else but me and no noise of any kind there. I looked at our sofa to make sure I was in the right place.

as I continued to grasp what I was doing there. I was placed in my past old house. Then, suddenly it came to me that I wanted to go to a Casino to play the slots. There were no Casino's in D C back then.

I then rushed out to my then old inoperative car. It started and I was on my way to a Maryland Casino that didn't exist even then. I was then in my early 20's when actually I was 77 years old. I could not stop for any signs, traffic lights, No other car in sight. After route 95 I was quickly at the Casino's parking lot. I quickly left the old car and was guided directly to the high-end slots. Then, instantly won the jackpot.

I don't remember driving back home to my Maryland apartment, but I must have by using my then much better 2004 car.

Payment for my finger 8 years earlier? All Via DIVINE POWER.

(Post-17)
Sometime early 2023

Some things don't just happen.

There is no big deal in even mentioning Fast Food restaurant. Since retirement I go there often. Of course, I know exactly what to expect once inside. I drive there each time, except that one time.

One day, I found myself standing tall in front of the wall inside the building waiting for my order. My thought was that I didn't order anything. The place was totally grayish in color and without people other than me. No employees to be seen. I was alone. Then, a cute young girl of about 7 years old in a red dress entered my sight She was accompanied by a very tall and muscular man. The girl walked directly beside him. I consider the man to be her father. They turned and stopped at the ordering section. Then, a little boy came into my view. He was in front of them. The boy was alone. They seemingly had to wait for the little boy to order first. The girl then looked up at her very tall muscular man who had nothing but scourging look toward the girl. I couldn't see her face her back was to me.

The girl breaks away from him and hop-skipped and jumped around the area. She then returns to stand again next to the man. She again looked up at him. He again indicated to her that he wanted nothing to do with her request of him or such. She again leaves her position and does another round of skips and jumps in the area. She quickly returned to stand next to him again. He refuses to look at her as she continues to look straight up at the man. She gives up and looks straight ahead. A very long wait for their food order as the little boy of about 5 was still ahead of them and making no headway.

Finally, I only think that I was given a food tray "ot my order". I was not holding, only an acting out the tray of ordered food. I didn't see any tables or chairs. I would have to go past the young girl in search for a table. Her back is to me as I was about to pass her, she quickly turned to face me with an ear-to-ear smile at me. I returned the same smile to her. She then instantly returned to be next to the man.

From that point on I have no clue what happened next.

It just seems a smile to be all she ever wanted from her father and would never get it. It could only be that my returned smile would satisfy her need for a smile from someone for the rest of her life.

No doubt I didn't have food, only a presumption of food. As in a piece of something in a make-believe food tray that I held in my hands. I left the "scene" knew not where I went next but had not taken a seat inside to enjoy my nothing. Another set up from DIVINE POWER?

The question is why? My only guess is that the DIVINE knew that the girl would keep bugging her father for a smile with her, Eventually, he would physically harm her. Maybe even kill her. My job was to satisfy her need of a smile with her, even if it came from a stranger and THE DIVINE.

Printed by Libri Plureos GmbH in Hamburg, Germany